The Q Guide to

Broadway

The Q Guides

FROM ALYSON BOOKS

POP CULTURE

Q

OUT THERE

·GUIDE

The Q Guide to

Broadway

**Stuff You Didn't Even Know You Wanted
to Know...**about the hits, flops,
the Tonys, and life upon the wicked stage

[seth rudetsky]

© 2006 BY SETH RUDETSKY

MANUFACTURED IN THE UNITED STATES OF AMERICA.

THIS TRADE PAPERBACK ORIGINAL IS PUBLISHED BY
ALYSON BOOKS
P.O. BOX 1253,
OLD CHELSEA STATION,
NEW YORK, NEW YORK 10113-1251

DISTRIBUTION IN THE UNITED KINGDOM BY
TURNAROUND PUBLISHER SERVICES
UNIT 3, OLYMPIA TRADING ESTATE
COBURG ROAD, WOOD GREEN
LONDON 722 6TZ ENGLAND.

FIRST EDITION: SEPTEMBER 2006

06 07 08 09 10 **a** 10 9 8 7 6 5 4 3 2 1

ISBN-10 1-55583-993-2
ISBN-13 978-1-55583-993-2

LIBRARY OF CONGRESS
CATALOGING-IN-PUBLICATION DATA IS ON FILE.

THEATRE PHOTOGRAPHS BY VICTOR MINGOVITS

This book is dedicated to everyone who has let me interview them. Thank you all for your candor, humor and details!

Contents

THE AUTHOR OF *THE Q GUIDE TO BROADWAY*, SETH RUDETSKY,
WITH *WILL & GRACE* ALUM (AND BROADWAY STAR OF *HOW
TO SUCCEED IN BUSINESS WITHOUT REALLY TRYING*) MEGAN
MULLALLY DURING A SEGMENT OF *SETH'S CHATTERBOX*.
(COURTESY OF FRANK CONWAY)

Introduction

HERE IS MY guide to all things Broadway.

Who am I?, you ask.

I'll field that one . . .

I'm Jean Valjea-a-a-a-a-a-a-an!

And so Javert you see–

Oh . . . sorry. I love quoting Broadway.

That's right, I'm one of those annoying people who is constantly referencing lyrics, musical phrases, facts, figures, dance steps, *and* scathing gossip. You see, I'm OBSESSED with Broadway! I've been this way my whole life. I literally have a reel-to-reel tape of myself belting up a storm before I turned three. Not childhood drivel like "Mary Had a Little Lamb," but the opening number from the Jo Sullivan/Robert Weede vehicle THE MOST HAPPY FELLA.

My parents got me hooked by introducing me to Broadway music and then taking me to see Broadway shows all throughout my childhood. Apparently they figured, "Why take Seth to the local production of SNOW WHITE when we can take him to the original Broadway run of HAIR? Who cares if he's only four years old? Yes, the nudity and drug references are a trifle mature, but Melba Moore's got it goin' on!"

I soon started spending all my free time in the den listening to show albums. I categorize my Broadway obsessions by what grade I was in. Second grade was THE PAJAMA GAME, third grade was CABARET, fourth grade was A CHORUS LINE, fifth grade was ANNIE, sixth grade was AIN'T MISBEHAVIN' (for a complete list, including what particular songs I listened to more than thirty times in a row, please email my Website and expect a long response).

The point is, once Broadway fever took hold, it never broke. I majored in piano at the Oberlin Conservatory and moved to New York hoping to be in a Broadway orchestra. I started as a piano sub at the short-lived MY FAVORITE YEAR (which I retitled "MY FAVORITE WEEK"), but I then went on to play in the pits of almost twenty Broadway musicals, including RAGTIME, PHANTOM OF THE OPERA, and KISS OF THE SPIDER WOMAN. Yet my obsession demanded more! I became an assistant conductor for the revival of GREASE, as well as THE PRODUCERS with Matthew Broderick and Nathan Lane.

But, still, I had to feed my addiction.

I realized I wanted to conduct the shows I had been obsessed with while I was growing up. I needed a time machine to take me back to when those shows were running so I could conduct that glorious music. I wasn't a fool, though. I knew that time machines only work in movies like *Back to the Future* and then get more and more boring with each sequel.

Suddenly, I had the answer! Since the shows I loved were closed, I'd open them up again! Working with The Actors' Fund of America, I started a once-a-year benefit concert series that raised money for the Fund using shows from my childhood obsessions. I got to conduct musicals like DREAMGIRLS and FUNNY GIRL, starring people like Josh Groban and Idina Menzel, and all the money raised went to the Actors' Fund.

I soon realized that I needed Broadway every minute of the day.

I had started hosting "Seth's Broadway Chatterbox," my weekly Broadway talk show in 1999, where I'd obsessively interview Broadway stars like John Lithgow and Megan Mullally for every detail of their careers, but I had to up the ante.

So, I started hosting my own Broadway radio show on SIRIUS Satellite radio seven days a week.

But I wasn't at peace.

Maybe I was lacking that old-time religion.

I decided to become a missionary. I needed to spread the gospel!

I took all those years of facts, figures, opinions, gossip, and dish with which I was saturated and poured them into this book! This is my bible, and I want to show you the way . . . the *Broad*way!

So come with me to find out hints like where to get great seats to the hottest "sold out" show, inside scoop like who had the worst job after winning a Tony Award, and a definitive list of what CDs you *must* own if you don't want to be laughed out of Joe Allen's. Start reading and soon you'll be able to impress/annoy your friends with more Broadway gossip than you can hear in the boy's dressing room at CHICAGO.

And those boys are *bitches*!

—*Seth Rudetsky, June 2006*

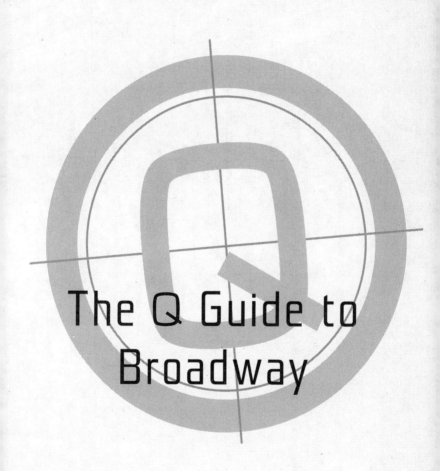

The Q Guide to Broadway

THE WINTER GARDEN THEATRE WAS THE HOME TO *CATS* FOR
EIGHTEEN YEARS, AND NOW HOSTS THE INTERNATIONAL
SMASH, *MAMMA MIA*. BY THE WAY, THE THEATRE'S OFFICIAL
NAME IS NOW THE CADILLAC WINTER GARDEN.

CHAPTER ONE

Broadway 101

 The definition of a Broadway theater simply has to do with how many seats there are.

THE WORD "Broadway" conjures up images of high-steppin' chorus boys, grandiose divas, and backstage bitchery.

Those images are accurate.

But there's a lot more to it. Let's start with the basics:

Broadway is a street that runs diagonally through Manhattan. It begins at Battery Park and ends in Washington Heights. The theater district begins where Broadway starts to cross through the West Forties. To the east of Broadway is Sixth Avenue, awkwardly titled "The Avenue of the Americas" and to the west is Eighth Avenue. Eighth Avenue used to be a red-light district, but Disney cleaned up the neighborhood and the hookers hoofed it farther west. Now if you want to see scantily clad ladies and gents shaking their business, get a ticket to CHICAGO.

A "Broadway theater" doesn't mean that the theater is located on Broadway. Actually, very few theaters are on Broadway proper. Most are on the side streets between Broadway and Eighth Avenue. The definition of a Broadway theater simply has to do with how many seats there are. If a professional theater in New York City has five hundred seats or more, it's a Broadway theater. That's the reason why both of the Lincoln Center theaters are housed in the same building, but the smaller Mitzi E. Newhouse Theater is considered Off-Broadway and the larger Vivian Beaumont is considered a Broadway house.

Most theaters are owned by producing organizations like the Jujamcyns or the Shuberts, or by not-for-profit companies like Manhattan Theatre Club or the Roundabout. The devastating news is that theaters are being renamed for corporations that give money. We used to only have theaters with Broadway-style names like The Palace or The Majestic or theaters that were named after great theatrical luminaries, like the Eugene O'Neill or the Barrymore. Now we have a huge theater on Forty-second Street with a name that's sure to make you think of greasepaint, divas, and hoofers: The American Airlines Theatre (note sarcasm). If only they could make it sound more corporate . . . but they can't. We've also seen the Winter Garden Theatre (home of WEST SIDE STORY and FUNNY GIRL) become the Cadillac Winter Garden Theatre, and in a demonstration of the whorishness of corporate Broadway, The Ford Center for the Performing Arts changed its name to The Hilton Theatre when it was purchased by Clear Channel. Not only are these names taking the Broadway out of Broadway, but by branding it so blatantly, there is the risk of artistic censorship. Will a big corporation be able to deal with a national boycott of its product if the theater named after it has a show deemed offensive to the "religious" right? Wouldn't the corporation find it easier to simply demand that the show take out the "objectionable" content? We shall see . . .

Back to less weightier issues. Broadway shows are mainly plays and musicals, but there are many different subgenres. There's the one-person autobiographical show like Billy Crystal's 700 SUNDAYS, the one-person comedy show like GILDA RADNER: LIVE FROM NEW YORK, the singing star concert/autobiography show like PATTI LUPONE LIVE, or the new dance play/musical like CONTACT or MOVIN' OUT. Then there are the shows that defy definitions like the recent BLAST, which consisted of elaborately dancing marching bands. Diverse as they are, all of these are Broadway shows. Essentially, if it's in a Broadway theater, it's a Broadway show.

Here's a brief history of Broadway mainstays.

Plays have been performed since time immemorial, but most Broadway plays in the eighteen hundreds were cheesy European imports about a hero, a villain, and a maiden that were acted in the "Victorian Style," like the silent movies of the 1900s. The 1920s brought us the great American playwrights whose works changed the broad acting of the nineteenth century to a style much more naturalistic (someone please tell Carol Channing).

Broadway musicals as we know them developed out of opera, Gilbert and Sullivan operetta, vaudeville, and burlesque. Most people consider SHOWBOAT (1927) to be the first American musical that combined music, drama, and dance to tell one story. OKLAHOMA!'s choreographer, Agnes DeMille, gets the credit for using dance not just to dress up the show but to advance the plot. In OKLAHOMA!, Laurey's "Out of My Dreams" ballet dramatically shows the conflict she's feeling between good-guy Curly and dark, dangerous, and slightly sexy Jud (not unlike my college diary entry dated October 5th, 1988, when I was torn between a good-natured T.A. and a "bad boy" oboe major.

In the old days, plays were just as popular as musicals. To this day, most people have heard of DEATH OF A SALESMAN, THE ODD COUPLE, and THE GLASS MENAGERIE. But, the names of current plays don't carry the weight of those titles (THE BLONDE IN THE THUNDERBIRD? Anybody?).

Many Broadway plays and musicals have been adapted from books, such as MAME (*Auntie Mame*), THE KING AND I (*Anna and the King of Siam*), and LES MISERABLES (or, LES MIZ as Broadway types refer to it), or from existing plays like THE MATCHMAKER (musicalized into HELLO, DOLLY!) or PYGMALLIAN (which became MY FAIR LADY). On the same continuum, Broadway plays and musicals have often been turned into films, but the success rate is not guaranteed. For every searing A STREETCAR NAMED DESIRE, there's a confusing headache like OLEANNA, and for every brilliant adaptation like the Oscar-winning CHICAGO, there's a devastatingly updated clunker like A CHORUS LINE.

Theater insiders complain about the trend nowadays to turn films into musicals, but that concept has been around for a long time. CARNIVAL is the musical version of the musical movie *Lily* (with totally different music). LITTLE SHOP OF HORRORS is based on the film of the same name, and Stephen Sondheim's A LITTLE NIGHT MUSIC was adapted from Bergman's *Smiles of a Summer Night*. I do agree, though, that lately we have had a deluge of hit movies trying to take Broadway by storm. Sometimes it works (THE PRODUCERS, HAIRSPRAY), and sometimes it's best never to speak of it again (SATURDAY NIGHT FEVER, URBAN COWBOY).

The newest trend to infiltrate Broadway is the "jukebox" musical. This entails taking music from one artist or composer (or even time period) and constructing a plot around it. Certain shows have been very successful doing it. Probably the most successful has been MAMMA MIA, which features the music of ABBA. They smartly included a story about a twenty-year-old pretty girl to appeal to young people (and straight men) and a story about a still-sexy forty-year-old and three of her ex-boyfriends, which appeals to the older crowd. Many shows have followed the trend set by MAMMA MIA, some successfully and some at an incredible loss (of money and dignity).

GOOD VIBRATIONS, featuring the music of The Beach Boys, is the butt of most jukebox-musical jokes. The show lacked a good plot (Will the nerdy girl become popular? Oh wait, she becomes popular...now what? Another act? You know what, don't wake me . . .), and the familiarity of the music wasn't enough to sustain it. It closed shortly after opening. Justin Guarini (from *American Idol*) did a previous incarnation of the show but dropped out before it came to Broadway. As to why he left, his lips were as tight as his perm.

After the failure of GOOD VIBRATIONS, the Broadway cognoscenti became very anti–jukebox musical. ALL SHOOK UP, which was a retelling of Shakespeare's TWELFTH NIGHT using the music of Elvis Presley, was the next jukebox musical to open after GOOD VIBRATIONS and, even though it was funny with great singing, it was pretty much written off by the press and the public because of the anti-jukebox vibe on Broadway.

Here's what people seem to forget. It's not the jukebox musical that is inherently bad, it's how it's executed. For instance, CRAZY FOR YOU was vaguely based on the old musical GIRL CRAZY but featured a 98-percent new plot and an array of music from the Gershwin library. In other words, a plot built around the music of a songwriting team. It wound up winning the 1992 Tony Award for best musical. I wonder, though, if it had opened right after GOOD VIBRATIONS, would people have rejected it and called it yet another jukebox musical? As a matter of fact, shows are now terrified of having the jukebox label attached to them. People associated with the Tony Award–winning JERSEY BOYS (the story and music of The Four Seasons) try to distance the show from that term, but the reality is JERSEY BOYS *is* a jukebox musical, it just happens to be a well-done one.

So, some jukebox musicals are hits and some are flops. But, what deems something a hit or a flop? There are many different definitions. From a commercial standpoint, it's solely based on whether the initial investment has been recouped. A show can run for years and still not recoup its investment. Likewise, a small show can have a limited run and pay back all of its investors. It all depends on the show's weekly "nut," meaning how much money is needed for advertising, actor salaries, theater rent, ushers, backstage crew, etc. . . .

Another way shows are judged is by reviews and public opinion. Some shows are critical favorites but public failures. PASSION won the Tony Award for best musical but ran for less than year, whereas JEKYLL AND HYDE got skewered by the critics but stayed on Broadway for almost five years!

Then there are the cult favorites. SIDE SHOW, a musical about conjoined twins, lasted for just one hundred performances, but its CD is coveted by musical-theater lovers. There are also legendary performances within flops. CARRIE is considered the biggest flop of the eighties, but Betty Buckley's performance as Carrie's mother was judged by some as the best of her brilliant career!

While there are many reviewers, *The New York Times* is still the one that matters the most. If you secure yourself a good *Times* review, you can be sure your show will run for awhile. Without the *Times*, you have to work *much* harder to get positive buzz for your show. SMOKEY JOE'S CAFE opened to mixed reviews but was kept alive with clever marketing and word of mouth. One device they employed happened during intermission. The producers made colorful SMOKEY JOE'S postcards available for the audience to fill out, hoping they would write about the great time they were having. SMOKEY JOE'S would collect the postcards, pay for the postage, and mail them. Scoff if you must, but that show ran for 2036 performances!

The Great White Way has changed a lot over the years. For one thing, the cost of a Broadway ticket has soared. In the mid-nineties, ticket prices hovered in the high sixty-dollar range but are now breaking one hundred dollars. In the past, Broadway shows didn't require such a big financial investment (top tickets cost around six dollars in 1938), so you were able to see a few shows a year without making a big dent in your bank account. Now, if a couple wants to see a Broadway show, they're not only paying for parking, dinner and a babysitter, but they have to shell out more than two hundred dollars just to get in to attend the performance. Because seeing a show is now such a big financial expenditure, people are reluctant to go unless they feel that they're guaranteed a good time. But how can that be guaranteed?

It used to be that a Broadway star's moniker above the title gave the audience a sense of security that the show they were going to see would be worth it. For instance, names like Ethel Merman, the Lunts, and John Raitt were big in the so-called "Golden Age" of Broadway (the thirties thru the sixties), but Broadway household names are much less prevalent today. Some of that has to do with financials. One of the ways producers have raised their profits is by eliminating the concept of "the Broadway star." It began with the marketing of show logos. Tourists didn't really know who was in LES MIZ or CATS, but they recognized the waif with the broom, or the cat's eyes, on the poster. Notice how the name of the star playing the Phantom is never in any advertisements, just the Phantom's mask. In other words, people are paying to see the show itself, not the person in it. Since the leading actors aren't the draw for the audience, the producers can pay them less.

There are still some Broadway names that can rake in the bucks. When tickets to THE ODD COUPLE starring Nathan Lane and Matthew Broderick went on sale, the show sold out instantly. Stars like them can negotiate special salary deals. Not only can they make around fifty thousand dollars a week or more (certainly higher than chorus minimum, which is around sixteen hundred dollars), they can also get a percentage of the tickets sales. The convential wisdom goes that if a star's name is what's selling tickets, that star should get a percentage of those tickets sold. No wonder *The Simpsons* (best show ever!) had a joke showing a Springfield theater district marquee that read:

Nathan Lane & Matthew Broderick
in
$$$$$$$$$$$$$$

The new Broadway star is the TV/film actor. Many producers feel secure that an actor whose name rings a bell will sell tickets. The Weisslers (ANNIE GET YOUR GUN, CHICAGO) are the producers who employ this method the most. When I did GREASE with them on Broadway, I walked through the stage door each night with a string of celebs that included Rosie O'Donnell, Debbie Boone, Joe Piscopo, Donny Most, Cousin Brucie, Sheena Easton, Jon Secada, Linda Blair, Chubbie Checker, Maureen McCormick, and Brooke

Shields over the course of its run.

Unfortunately, while some of the "name" stars who come to Broadway are fierce, others are not up to snuff as theater actors, but their names sell tickets. There have been some great turns by TV/film/pop-star actors on Broadway (Antonio Banderas was brilliant in NINE, Reba McEntire gave an incredible performance in ANNIE GET YOUR GUN), but there have also been some embarrassing nachtmares (Faye Dunaway sang so badly at the rehearsal for SUNSET BOULEVARD they had to close the production before she opened in it!).

All in all, there is *no way* to guarantee a successful show. Well, you say, how about a well-known creative team, a well-known product, and two bona fide stars? THE GOODBYE GIRL had lyrics by David Zippel, who wrote the successful CITY OF ANGELS, and music by Marvin Hamlisch, who had won three Oscars and composed what was for a time the longest-running musical, A CHORUS LINE. The show was based on a popular Neil Simon movie and starred Tony Award–winner Bernadette Peters and *Saturday Night Live* alum Martin Short.

It lasted five months.

On the other hand, AVENUE Q was an off-Broadway show with a small cast and no chorus. It had no stars and no elaborate set, but it transferred to Broadway, got great reviews, and won the Tony Award for best musical!

Another thing that's changed is the popularity of Broadway music. In the old days, if a Broadway show was a hit, it usually had at least one song that would get on the pop charts. Doris Day recorded THE PAJAMA

GAME's "Hey There," Louis Armstrong made "Hello, Dolly!" a hit, and even The Beatles recorded MUSIC MAN's "Till There Was You." That radically changed in the late 1960s when musical tastes evolved and the Broadway sound remained old school. Unfortunately, the American public today is so ignorant of Broadway music that many people think Gwen Stefani wrote her hit song, "If I Was a Rich Girl."

She didn't. The hook is from FIDDLER ON THE ROOF. (On a side note: I understand why she changed the word "man" to "girl," but why couldn't she have sung "if I *were* a rich girl"? Is the subjunctive considered "not cool"?)

All in all, though Broadway isn't the way it used to be, it still has fans all over the world, and it's one of the best things New York has to offer. Millions of people see Broadway shows each year, generating billions of dollars in tickets sales, not to mention merchandising and CDs. This was your introduction to Broadway. Now let's start dishing!

THE EPONYMOUS BROADWAY THEATRE. *LES MISERABLES* FIRST
PLAYED HERE BEFORE IT MOVED TO THE IMPERIAL, GIVING
WAY FOR THE TEN-YEAR RUN OF *MISS SAIGON*. *THE COLOR
PURPLE* TOOK UP RESIDENCE IN 2006.

CHAPTER TWO

Broadway-insider Lingo

Understudy does not mean under-talented. Lots of fabulously talented people have understudied.

HAVE YOU ever hung out with a group of theater people and felt like an idiot? You were probably barraged with sentences like "He said he's swinging that show, but I spoke to the MD about it and he told me the track is open" and nodded with a Paris Hilton vapidity in your eyes. With this chapter's help, you can talk the talk, walk the walk, and bitch the bitch with anyone from out-of-work chorus boy to multiple Tony Award winner.

Stage Right/Stage Left

This means either the right or left from the perspective of the actor. It prevents the annoyance of directors having to say, "Go right. No, *my* right." You may think this term is obvious, but I was once rehearsing with a TV star who was transplanted to Broadway and after a *full day* of staging she finally asked, "Um . . . what's stage left?" I won't reveal her name but will tell you that her show was post–*The Courtship of Eddie's Father* and pre–*Silver Spoons*.

Track

A role in a show isn't called a role anymore amongst the Broadway elite. It's called a "track." Once a show is up and running, it's easy to break down what a person does into what their movement is (enter stage right, do opening number, exit stage left, do a quick change, do a crossover and move set piece, sing backup vocals from backstage mic, etc.). Essentially, every actor is following an invisible track. So when people go into a show that's running, they'll say, "I'm doing Joanne Hunter's track," meaning they're doing the part Joanne originated.

Sub

A musician's understudy is called a sub, as in substitute. The musicians' union allows musicians to miss 50 percent of their performances. In other words, a musician can miss four shows out of an eight-show week. This is because musicians are always gigging recording sessions, weddings, jazz clubs, etc. You may think that fifty percent is a lot to be allowed to miss compared to the actor who has to make a special request for a personal day (wedding, funeral, etc.), but when you go to see FIDDLER ON THE ROOF, you'd be pretty upset if the Tevye understudy is on, but you probably won't burst into tears if you notice there's a different piccolo player in the pit. Let's be honest: there are no "name" orchestra players, so as long as the sub is good, the audience doesn't care.

To be a sub, you obviously have to learn the part you're subbing for. Then you have to do a performance of the show *with no rehearsal*. You don't have a "put-in" rehearsal like an actor does. The really scary part is that your first performance is also your audition! If you don't play well, you're not "asked back." The pressure is enormous.

Actors say they can tell when it's a sub's first time playing, especially when it's a trumpet player. Often the last note of a finale is a high trumpet note, and when a trumpet cracks, it's *mucho* obvious. And hilarious. Usually, onstage there'll be some subtle eye rolls if someone is clanking it up in the pit, but sometimes actors have a harsher reaction. One Broadway diva felt the sub drummer missed the sassy accents in her big number, and after she finished her dance, she walked over to him and kicked a hole in his bass drum with her high-heeled dance shoes!

The Music Staff

A Broadway musical has a whole music staff that works on all aspects of the music.

Music director

Often called the "MD" in Broadway lingo, the music director is in charge of shaping all of the music. First the MD works with the performers to pick the right keys for the songs. For instance, when SWEENEY TODD was revived with Patti LuPone, the music director took down some keys. Angela Lansbury's keys were higher and helped convey her flighty portrayal of Mrs. Lovett; Patti's choice was to be a sexier Mrs. Lovett, which sounded better in a lower key. Plus this SWEENEY TODD was a much more intimate affair. Patti was able to keep it smaller by making the keys lower.

The music director works with the theatrical director while the show is being created. Since the music director is at every rehearsal and the composer is not, the MD is the liason between the composer and the director. Does a scene need underscoring to get an emotional point across? The director tells the MD who tells the composer what is needed (in certain shows, the MD will write it instead of the composer). Although one might think that once a score is written, it stays as is, one would be mistaken. A score to a show is constantly having sections added and subtracted, under the helm of the music director. Sometimes, more music is needed to cover a costume or a scene change. For instance, the whole section in "Springtime for Hitler" with Winston Churchill and Franklin Delano Roosevelt was created after the song was written to cover a set change behind the curtain. That was a process that occurred between the MD, the composer, and the director.

The MD also usually conducts the show. That means being in charge of tempos. In dance shows, that's particularly important. What's merely difficult at one tempo can lead to a broken leg at another tempo.

The conductor also works with the singers to

interpret the songs. They work out what the journey of the song is, when to breathe, when to vibrato, when to bring it down, when to sing full out, what sounds off pitch, etc.

The conductor not only leads the orchestra and singers but has a big part in the pacing of a show. One of the jobs of the conductor is the timing of laughs. Sometimes music comes right after a laugh line, and the conductor has to know when to bring it in so the music doesn't cut off the laugh before it's had a chance to peak, or worse, the laugh doesn't pathetically die out in silence. Same thing with applause. No actor wants his applause cut off before it's time, but they also don't want to be standing on stage as the applause dwindles to a smattering of pity claps. It's up to the conductor to decide what feels right.

Arranger

Musicals require someone to write their song and/or vocal arrangements. Sometimes a composer does the vocal arrangements (Stephen Flaherty, who wrote RAGTIME, always does), and sometimes the music director does or someone else is brought on. Vocal arrangements can make or break a song. Take "Oklahoma!". If the song were just the melody it would be enjoyable, but what makes the number fantastic is the vocal arrangement. Listen to when the tenors sing that long arpeggiated "sky-y-y-y" right before the bridge. Fabulous! One of the other great arrangements in that song is when they all start harmonizing "Okla, Okla, homa, homa" and then one group keeps chanting with that part and the other group takes over the melody. So exciting!!!!

A song arranger takes the song the composer wrote and arranges it. For instance, "'T ain't Nobody's Bizness If I Do" is a hot, uptempo number in AIN'T MISBEHAVIN', but it has a slow, bluesy groove in the show BLACK AND BLUE. It's still the same notes and chord changes, but it's a totally different arrangement.

Orchestrator

The orchestrator takes the accompaniment the composer/arranger wrote and divides it between the instruments of the orchestra. To hear some brilliant orchestration, listen to a Sondheim show. Jonathan Tunick is one of the best. A great example is "A Weekend in the Country" from A LITTLE NIGHT MUSIC. At the very end, the singers hold a big chord and the French horn plays a triumphant fanfare. It's thrilling! Or listen to something subtle like "If They Could See Me Now" from SWEET CHARITY (the original!). Ralph Burns has the violins playing fast sixteenth notes every measure to keep the song moving. You may not realize how much you're aware of the orchestration. You know the part in "Do, Re, Mi" when the kids and Maria finally add words to the tune they made up? There is a flute line that plays in the background that you can probably hum but never realized you could. Have a listen and see if I'm right!

One of the sad things that's happening on Broadway is that orchestrators are being forced to orchestrate for smaller and smaller orchestras. Why is it that Broadway prices are higher than ever, but orchestras are smaller? Find a show that has been revived and listen to the first version and then the revival. The original orchestras are big and delicious, and the revival orchestras have cut a ton of instruments and replaced them with tacky synthesizers. Shouldn't Broadway have full orchestras? Where is the money going from ticket sales? Certainly not to a string section. Nowadays, you're lucky if there's a string quartet in a Broadway show. If you feel strongly about this, make your voice heard! Bring the full orchestras back to Broadway! Musicals shouldn't sound worse than they did in the fifties, they should sound better!

Stage Managers

Stage managers are in charge of the whole show. They are there at every rehearsal and have to know how every facet works. The lighting, the set, the music, the actors . . . the stage manager is the leader. They're in charge of calling breaks for the actors during rehearsals (five minutes every hour, ten every hour and a half), and they also take notes so they can rehearse the actors, understudies, and replacements when the director isn't there. During the show, they're in charge of calling the cues. In the old days, it was mostly lighting cues, but nowadays it also includes all the computerized stage craft that is constantly being developed. When the curtain goes up or comes down, the stage manager gives the cue. When the chandelier falls during PHANTOM OF THE OPERA or the house collapses during AN INSPECTOR CALLS, the stage manager gives the cue.

Stage managers have to know something about music because lots of cues are within a song. They must understand how to count music so they can cue the light change on the fifteenth-and-a-half beat of a dance break. Usually, they're standing right offstage, wearing a headset that goes to the electricians, the spot operator, the person in charge of the turntable, the sound operators, etc., and they call cues constantly.

Lights cue 127B stand by.

Go!

Sound effects cue 3 stand by.

Center spotlight cue 15 stand by.

Go! Go!

One famous debacle happened during a musical that was trying to sell more tickets by bringing in a woman who had no experience performing but had a name people recognized. It was her first night on a Broadway stage, nay, her first night on *any* stage. She was waiting backstage fifteen minutes before she had to make her first entrance. The stage manager had a lighting cue to call and said "Go!" The actress heard the directive, thought it was for her, and stumbled out on stage into a scene where she did not belong. She looked around at actors she wasn't used to seeing, realized she was fourteen minutes early, and tiptoed back offstage.

Gypsy

This was coined during the golden age of Broadway. In the forties and fifties, Broadway shows were always opening, and if you were a chorus person, you could go from one to another all the time. You were constantly traveling just like a Gypsy, so the phrase "Broadway gypsy" was born. Nowadays, European Gypsies prefer to be called "Roma," but the Broadway folk like to kick it old school.

Substitutes

Understudy

We've all heard the term "understudy," but what actually is it? Understudies in a play are a little different from understudies in a musical. In a musical, an understudy is someone who performs in a show eight times a week (either chorus or featured role) and is also prepared to perform another, usually bigger, part. A play usually has a smaller cast, so often the understudy is like a standby, i.e., they're only onstage if they're going on a for another actor.

Understudy does not mean under-talented. Lots of fabulously talented people have understudied. For example, in the 1986 revival of SWEET CHARITY, Bebe Neuwirth won a Tony Award for portraying the sassy sidekick, Nicki, but she also understudied Debbie Allen, who played the leading role of Charity. Two-time Tony Award–winner Donna Murphy was in the chorus of THE MYSTERY OF EDWIN DROOD but understudied Betty Buckley, who played the title role.

It's a union rule that every role in a Broadway show has to have an understudy. A Broadway musical usually has a cast of at least twenty people, but there aren't twenty extra people serving as understudies. More often than not, understudies cover multiple roles. Hopefully, there are enough understudies to go around. But it's not very rare for there to be a shortage of understudies. When that happens, people are juggled around. In A CHORUS LINE, one understudy went on for two different roles *during the same performance.* Both performers were out, and it so happened that they were playing the two roles that she understudied. She just sort of combined both characters lines and vocal solos and fortunately didn't have to worry about entrances and exits because everyone in that show is onstage pretty much the whole time.

When I was doing GREASE, we had so many people out sick one night, that we ran out of understudies. Act Two usually began with a quartet singing tight four-part harmony. On that night, we opened with a trio instead, and a major harmony line was left out. Although, thinking back, that was the least of that revival's problems!

Of course, the most famous understudy of them all is Shirley MacLaine. She was a mere twenty-year-old chorus dancer in the 1954 production of THE PAJAMA GAME. It was her second Broadway show, and besides dancing in the chorus, she was also the understudy to Carol Haney, who played Gladys. The role of Gladys not only had lots of comedy lines, but she also got to dance and sing the famous "Steam Heat" number in Act Two (choreographed by a young Bob Fosse). Actors' Equity (the actors' union) requires that every role has an understudy, but everybody involved in the production knew that Carol Haney never missed a performance. That is, until the day that Carol broke her leg!

Shirley got to the theater (fifteen minutes late because of a subway breakdown!) and was immediately told she was going on that night as Gladys. Even though she never had a real rehearsal, she wound up getting big laughs in all the right places during Act One and got through STEAM HEAT in Act Two (even though she dropped her hat and said "Shit!" onstage).

Lo and behold, just like in a movie, there happened to be a Hollywood producer named Hal B. Wallis in the audience that night who came backstage and offered her a screen test. Soon she was starring in the Alfred Hitchcock movie THE TROUBLE WITH HARRY. Just like Peggy Sawyer in 42nd Street, the cliché of the understudy who becomes a star came true!

If it weren't for the Equity rule that every role must have an understudy, we probably never would have gotten to see Shirley MacLaine's brilliant performances in *Steel Magnolias, Terms of Endearment,* and *Postcards from the Edge.* Then again, if it weren't for that rule, we would have been spared the clunker *Evening Star* and a mélange of eighties New Age books.

Standby

Every role must have an understudy, but a standby is a luxury only certain shows have. A standby is usually hired if the star of the show is particularly famous or if the role is unusually difficult. For instance, Nathan Lane (big star) had a standby in A FUNNY THING HAPPENED ON THE WAY TO THE FORUM. The role of Elphaba in WICKED, which is extremely difficult to sing, also has a standby.

You may ask, "Why an understudy *and* a standby?" Well, usually you can get a more experienced actor to be a standby because it's a little more prestigious than being an understudy. Even though conceivably the actor may never go on, he/she can still haughtily say, à la MAME's Vera Charles, " I was never in the chorus." (At least for that show.) That's because understudies toil in the chorus eight shows a week if they're not going on for the role they understudy, but a standby literally stands by. At first, they're in the audience watching and learning the role that they're covering, but once they know it, they're free to do whatever they want. If you wander backstage while a show is being performed, you'll see the standby hanging out and playing Boggle, Scrabble, watching TV, reading, knitting, etc. Also, many standbys have a contract that allows them to go within five blocks of the theater as long as they're on beeper or cell phone. That's in case of an emergency during the show. There has been many a standby who was eating dinner, suddenly been beeped, and apologetically said, "Sorry. You can have my side salad. I have to go star in a Broadway show."

FAMOUS STANDBY LORE

Idina Menzel injured herself during her second-to-last performance of WICKED, so her standby, Shoshana Bean, did what was supposed to be Idina's final performance. Even though Shoshanna was fierce, the audience was disappointed because they had all bought tickets hoping to see Idina's last hurrah. So, Idina, clad in a red tracksuit because her rib was injured, came out and performed the final scene in the show to tumultuous applause. There is now a tradition in WICKED that when an Elphaba leaves the show, she gets a red tracksuit.

Swing

Do you ever stay till the end of a movie and see the job titles that sound bizarre? Do you sit there and think, *What's a gaffer? And what the hell is a best boy? Does he charge for full release*? I'm sure a lot of people feel the same thing when they read a *Playbill* and see people in the cast listed as "swing." Here's the deal: "Swing" is not the name of a character. A swing is someone who understudies the ensemble. Usually one man for the male ensemble and one woman for the female. The name swing comes from the fact that they can swing from role to role. You may think, *What's the hard part? A swing understudies people in the background. It's more difficult to understudy a real part.* The truth is that being a swing is *très difficile.* First of all, most ensembles sing in harmony. That means the male swing has to know all the vocal parts of every guy in the ensemble. Not just bass and tenor, but often there are three different tenor parts and three different bass parts. Same thing for the female swing. Then they have to know everybody's staging. The whole stage is set up like a grid. When you go see a Broadway show, try to look at the very front of the stage. (This is easier if you're in the balcony with opera glasses . . . if you walk to the front of the stage, usually the orchestra pit separates you from the stage.) There are numbers, spaced out evenly, written across the front perimeter. There are also wings, or openings, on the sides of the stage that lead to backstage. Actors use the combination of both to know where they're supposed to be on stage. Wing 1, number 8, stage left. This system is used to keep the actors in their light and to prevent them from bumping into people onstage with them. Of course, there is freedom to move around during a scene or solo, but dances have to be much more specific. A typical dancer says to themselves, "I start the first turn on number 3, stage left, wing 1; do a jeté to number 5, stage right; do five chaîné turns that lead me to number 7, stage left, and exit at wing 2." Each dancer has different numbers to mark where they're supposed to be during a song. A swing has to know all of them. Plus, a lot of times the ensemble is in charge of stage business, like unhooking Galinda from her bubble in WICKED or taking Christine out of her rehearsal skirt and into her performance outfit before "Think of Me" in THE PHANTOM OF THE OPERA.

The swing usually keeps a "show bible" that has every single character and all of his/her numbers and staging in it. The swing will usually check it right before a song to make sure he/she knows what numbers to land on, what props to remember, and what solos they have. And often, a swing will go on for one dancer during the matinee and then go on for a totally different one for the night show. The swing has to be able to keep all those different numbers/props/harmonies/etc. straight. Most of them have an architectural mind, so they're able to see the big picture of stage and where they fit in on the grid. Not checking to see what number you're on can lead to a sloppy performance and/or a MAJOR mishap!

Jim Borstelmann who is a fabulous dancer (CHICAGO) and comedian (THE PRODUCERS) was the swing in JEROME ROBBINS' BROADWAY, his first Broadway show. He was so excited to finally get to go on that he wasn't checking his numbers when he performed "The Rumble" during the WEST SIDE STORY segment. He was a little off from where he was supposed to be, so when he turned his head quickly, he smashed it into a pole and broke his tooth, which was expelled through his lip! With his tooth sitting on the stage and blood pouring out of his lip, he still had the dancer mentality that the show must go on, and he finished the number. When Jim exited the stage, he looked down at his costume, a white T-shirt and jeans, and saw that the T-shirt had turned bright red because he had bled all over it. The capper is that as he was leaving the theater during intermission to be taken to the hospital, he overheard an audience member saying, " 'The Rumble' seemed so realistic. Is it like that every night?"

•

SO, NOW you know your terms. Get thee to Joe Allen (a restaurant popular with the theatre elite) and strike up a conversation with a gypsy. Ask what his or her "track" is and if they like their "stage manager". Maybe you can come up with an "arrangement" with them that ends with you "swinging" till dawn. Or maybe you'll just be an "understudy" till their boyfriend or girlfriend shows up, and you're left sitting at the bar with a half-empty cosmo and a dogeared copy of this book.

QUIZ

Know Your Sondheim

1. Who lived near the young Stephen Sondheim and mentored his musical theater writing?

   a. *Richard Rodgers*
   b. *Oscar Hammerstein II*
   c. *Lorenz Hart*
   d. *Pink*

2. Name two Sondheim shows (music and lyrics) that Angela Lansbury starred in.

3. Name the actors who played the title role in Broadway's SWEENEY TOOD from the original, the revival in 1989, and the revival in 2005.

4. What show did Sondheim write to be performed in the swimming pool at Yale and later starred Nathan Lane?

Know Your Sondheim

5. Who played Desirée in the movie
   version of A LITTLE NIGHT MUSIC?

   A. *Liz Taylor*
   B. *Barbra Streisand*
   C. *Glynis Johns*
   D. *Paris Hilton and Nicole Ritchie
      (one of them got bored halfway
      through filming)*

THIRD TIME'S THE CHARM FOR THE AMBASSADOR THEATRE. THE LONG-RUNNING REVIVAL OF *CHICAGO* MOVED HERE FROM THE SHUBERT AFTER ORIGINALLY OPENING AT THE RICHARD RODGERS.

CHAPTER THREE

How to Snag a Ticket and Navigate Broadway

Q FACT

Seeing a show in previews allows you to really form an opinion about a show free from what you're "supposed" to think.

How To Choose a Show

You're coming to New York and you want to see a fabulous Broadway show. Of course you do, you're gay. (Or not . . . not that there's anything wrong with that. Hey, Broadway is for everyone!) But how do you decide what to see?

There's nothing worse than spending full price for something (around one hundred dollars) and then hating it. Believe me, I know. I saw *Waterworld* opening weekend. (I know it was only seven dollars, not one hundred, but I was artistically traumatized for two hours out of my life. That's worth at least the remaining ninety-three bucks.)

Now, many people come to New York and say, "I heard of (blank). Let's see that. It must be good, since I've heard of it."

That theory doesn't fly. Hearing of something doesn't "make it good." I myself have heard of having all my wisdom teeth pulled, but that doesn't make it good (except the "milkshake only" recovery diet). Essentially, an out-of-towner hears about most shows due mainly to constant commercials and print ads. All that means is said show has a lot of money in its advertising budget, not that the show is good.

For instance, IN MY LIFE, which got some of the worst reviews in Broadway history, was written, directed, and produced by the man who made millions from writing "You Light Up My Life." He poured thousands of dollars into commercials that put the name of the show into the heads of unsuspecting patrons, who came to New York, saw the marquee, and said, "I've heard of that; it must be good." To say that most were sorely disappointed after seeing it is like saying Chita Rivera was sorely disappointed when Rita Moreno got the role of Anita in the movie version of WEST SIDE STORY and subsequently won the Oscar.

So, how do you decide what to see?

1. Watch the Tonys each year. All nominated musicals get to perform a number. If you like the number, you have a good chance of liking the show.

2. Go to iTunes and download a couple of songs from possible shows you want to see. It's only ninety-nine cents per song, and it will give you the gist of whether the music is up your alley. If the show is a revival or has a London as well as a Broadway cast, make sure you download the correct version of the show! The original "Brotherhood of Man" from the sixties version of HOW TO SUCCEED IN BUSINESS WITHOUT REALLY TRYING is nothing compared to the revival version. The revival version sassed up the arrangement for Lillias White, who brought the house down. Similarly, Patti LuPone (who only did SUNSET BOULEVARD in London) performs a version of "With One Look" that is amazing compared to the sounds emitted by Glenn Close.

3. Ask your friends who see shows! Obviously, there are many different opinions out there (for instance, some people love Glenn Close's "singing"), but a consensus can't be wrong (unless it's a national election).

4. Go online! You can Google old reviews and go to the many different theater chat boards to read opinions and ask questions (see chat boards, Chapter Four).

5. Go in blind! Take a chance and see a show in previews. Before a show opens for the critics, it previews on Broadway for a few weeks to get itself into shape. Songs are put in, scenes are rearranged, jokes are added, etc. until the show is as perfect as it's gonna get. Seeing a show in previews allows you to really form an opinion about a show free from what you're "supposed" to think. There are no critics' raves/pans and/or award nominations or lack thereof to

influence you. And, the truth is, most people are very easily influenced. When BABY (a musical by Maltby and Shire) first opened, audiences were fairly responsive, but not overly so. When it was nominated for a Tony Award for best musical and best score, the show suddenly began to get standing ovations every night. Not because the show was any different, but because audiences knew the show had been lauded. Same show, different reaction.

So, go see a preview. Even if you hate it overall, there's always *something* to like about a show. RAGS (four performances) had Judy Kuhn belting out one of the best title songs ever; Lar Lubavitch's ballet in Act Two of THE RED SHOES (28 performances) was breathtaking; Kristin Chenoweth won a Tony Award for her part in the short-lived YOU'RE A GOOD MAN, CHARLIE BROWN.

And if the show you see is truly awful, you can become part of theater lore. When someone in a group of theater cognoscenti mentions Farrah Fawcett's BOBBIE BOLAND, which had seven performances and never officially opened, the person that can say "I saw it" is instantly a celebrity. *You* can be that person for the next train wreck to hit Broadway! And remember, there really is no show that is universally reviled. You may be in the small percentage that absolutely loved DANCE OF THE VAMPIRES or GOOD VIBRATIONS! (If you are, put this book down immediately and start reprogramming yourself by listening to the original cast albums of WEST SIDE STORY and A CHORUS LINE.)

Tickets

Once you decide on a show you want to see, you need to get tickets. If you don't mind paying full price and you're near the theater district, you can use the box office, that way you won't have to pay the extra costs the online ticket services add on. Go to the theater of the show you want to see and ask for tickets for the date you want. Sometimes when a show is sold out, because seats are held for VIPs, tickets can become available at the last minute, so it's worth a shot. Here are some other ways:

Broadway Inner Circle

If money is no object and you're willing to spend a lot, you can pretty much see whatever you want, whenever you want. It used to be the only way to get tickets to the hottest shows on Broadway at the last minute was through a scalper who would sell you one at an outrageously inflated price. Now producers have become the scalper! Uh . . . I mean, producers have figured out a way to make scalpers obsolete. They've created an organization called The Broadway Inner Circle, which you can access at www.broadwayinnercircle.com. Or call 1-866-847-8587. Prices start at more than double a regularly priced ticket and range from $250 to $480. But, these seats are "house seats" meaning they're the best seats in the house. So if you're a gazzilionaire, it's a guaranteed way to get a great seat.

Brokers

You can also buy from ticket brokers who mark up the price of tickets as well. It's *très cher*, but if you're desperate to see the big, sold-out hit of the season and you can only go on a certain night, it's worth it.

Here is a partial list:

TicketsNow–www.tickets.com
Go Tickets–www.gotickets.com
Broadway Shows.org–www.broadwayshows.org

And for group sales:

Broadway.com–www.broadway.com/groups
Best of Broadway–www.bestofbroadway.com

But if you have that kind of money, why don't you give some of it to charity *and* see a Broadway show. Sound impossible? If you believe in fairies, keep reading.

The Good Karma Way

The first place to go when you need tickets is two wonderful Broadway charities.

THE ACTORS' FUND OF AMERICA

The name of the Actors' Fund is actually a misnomer. This amazing charity is for *anybody* in the arts (writers, dancers, ushers, stagehands, musicians, etc.) and provides numerous services such as a free health clinic, as well as money for rent, medical bills or any other need. They also own two homes for the elderly on each coast. The Actors' Fund has access to two pairs of tickets to every Broadway show for every performance. The great news is the tickets are tax deductible! But remember, they must be ordered at least forty-eight hours in advance by phone at 212-221-7300 x111, or for you out-of-towners, 1-800-FUNDTIX x111.

BROADWAY CARES/EQUITY FIGHTS AIDS (BC/EFA)

BC/EFA is a wonderful group that raises money for AIDS organizations all over the world. If you want tix to a sold out show in New York, or even in other parts of the country, there are usually seats available through Care Tix. They're sold at double the face value (which is still cheaper than Broadway Inner Circle and the mark up is tax deductible) and the money goes to BC/EFA, which gives away millions in grants to big groups like GMHC and little ones like Alabama's Meals on Wheels.

TDF

If you are looking for discounts, you should check out TDF, which stands for Theatre Development Fund. It was formed to promote live theater and they administer a mailing list that's fabulous. If you're a student, teacher, union member, retiree, civil service employee, nonprofit organization staff member, member of the clergy or armed service, or a performing-arts professional (in other words, if you're alive), you are eligible to get on the mailing list. It's a monthly publication that offers pages of Broadway/off-Broadway, music, and dance tickets at fifty to seventy-five percent off! Even if you only use it once, it's worth the $22.50 annual fee. All you have to do is send a stamped, self-addressed envelope (with proof that you belong to one category on the eligibility list) to TDF, 1501 Broadway, twenty-first floor, New York, New York 10036-5652. You can also get an application at www.tdf.org.

TKTS

The Theatre Development Fund also runs TKTS. For some reason, the name of this half-price ticket booth has taken the word "tickets" and discarded the vowels and the letter *c*. Wouldn't it have been easier to call it "Tickets"? If the name was derived to save time, it backfired. By the time I say "T-K-T-S," I could have said the word "tickets" two-and-a-half times.

Regardless, this is an easy and cheap way to see a Broadway show that's not at its height of popularity. All you have to do is show up, wait on line, and you will have a choice of a ton of Broadway and off-Broadway plays and musicals. The downside is that waiting on line can take more than an hour. Generally, the closer you get to showtime, the shorter the line. So if you don't want to wait, get there around twenty minutes before show time, and you'll be in and out in minutes. And actually, sometimes a hit show will release tickets late in the day, so you may have a better chance at snagging a hard-to-get ticket than someone who got there super early. Usually, the tickets are 50 percent off. Some of the more popular shows are only discounted 25 percent. Tickets at the midtown location (Forty-seventh Street and Broadway) are only available the day of the performance. The hours are:

> Monday to Friday – 3:00 p.m. to 8:00 p.m.
> Wednesday and Saturday matinees –10:00 a.m. to
> 2:00 p.m.
> Sunday matinees – 11:00 a.m. to 3:00 p.m.
> Sunday evenings – 3:00 p.m. to close

There is also a location downtown at the South Street Seaport (South Street Seaport, 199 Water Street, at the corner of Front and John Streets), and the benefit of going there is that it opens at eleven o'clock in the morning for the evening performances and matinee tickets are available the *day before*. The hours are:

> Monday to Friday – 3:00 p.m. to 8:00 p.m.
> Wednesday and Saturday matinees – 10:00 a.m. to
> 2:00 p.m.
> Sunday matinees – 11:00 a.m. to 3:00 p.m.
> Sunday evenings – 3:00 p.m. to close

Standing Room

Standing-room tickets are not what everyone thinks they are. First of all, the good part is they're cheap! Usually twenty-five dollars. The bad part is not every Broadway theater has space for standing room. Also, you can't just go to any show that has standing room and get a ticket. They usually won't sell the standing room until the show is sold out. Now, if you wind up getting a standing-room ticket, understand that it's not like the riffraff room on *Ellen*, i.e., it's not a separate room that you watch the show from. It's in the orchestra section of the audience (usually), right behind the last row. Whatever you do, don't forget your distance glasses, and if you have opera glasses, bring 'em!

Where you stand is not a free-for-all. There are numbers assigned to each standing area to avoid jockeying for the best spot. You don't have to stand with your hands plastered at your side, though. You lean over the wall in back of the last row of seats, and the top of the wall is padded so you can rest your arms there. It's actually kind of comfortable except for the incredible strain on the knees and gams. Make sure you walk around during intermission to get the circulation back in your legs! And don't wear high heels! If you want to look sassy, arrive at the theater in stilettos, but do what a seasoned secretary does on the subway: put on a pair of sneakers! You can sass out again as you leave the theater.

Even though a show is sold out, it doesn't necessarily mean that everyone will show up, so it pays to suck up to an usher. Many times, they take pity on the standees and let them sit in a seat that's remained empty. Sometimes, though, if you snag a seat without asking, the real seat holder will arrive late and you'll be busted. There's nothing more mortifying than being forced to relinquish a seat you were too cheap to buy! It always involves an usher's glaring flashlight, a fumble for your pathetic standing-room ticket, and a march of shame to the back of the orchestra section where your fellow standees haughtily smirk at you.

Rush Seats

Rush seats stand for a new trend on Broadway that makes cheap seats available by a lottery. RENT was the trendsetter because the author, Jonathan Larson, only made a waiter's salary. He had always wanted a way to make Broadway accessible to people like him, so every performance of RENT has twenty-dollar tickets available for the first two rows of the theater. When it first opened, people would camp out on the sidewalk all night because the tickets were given out first come/first serve, but now there's a lottery. You just sign up for the tix (two maximum) starting two-and-a-half hours before the show, and they'll draw the names at two hours before curtain.

Different shows have different policies. Some of them only allow you to get rush seats if you're a student, but all of them require ID when you pick up your tickets. They don't want someone signing up a million times under various pseudonyms. The best way to find out how each show's rush policy works is to go to talkinbroadway.com (see Chapter Four). And don't be discouraged if you don't get seats the first time. I have many friends that have gotten into the hottest shows with rush tickets. If you're going by yourself, sign up for two tickets anyway. There's bound to be someone there who wants the extra rush ticket. And, who knows, they might appreciate the "rush" seat so much, they'll take you out after the show for some coffee! But, even if they're super attractive, take my advice . . . don't "rush" into a relationship!

HAHAHAHA! Don't you love puns? I'm laughing so hard I can hardly type.

Hmmm . . . why do I sense silence coming from my reader?

ALTERNATE METHODS

There are many other ways to get a ticket. With the advent of theater message boards, you can simply post a plea for a ticket with your email address. Shoppin' Broadway (part of talkinbroadway.com) is where people sell Broadway tickets usually at a discount or for "best offer." It's a great place to stop by first whenever you're looking to see a show. You never know when someone bought a ticket to the new big Broadway hit, can't get a babysitter, and is being forced to sell it.

Also, every cast member of a Broadway show usually has access to the best seats in the house called "house seats." So use your connections! Do you know anyone who knows *anyone* on Broadway? Once someone is on Broadway, they always know someone connected to every show. Find out if they'll get you house seats. You'll pay full price, but you'll be in a primo seat. If you don't know anyone, feel free to suck up in a letter! Send a letter to a chorus person/star/stage manager explaining how much you want to see the show, and ask if there's any way they'll get you a house seat. The worse that will happen is you'll get a restraining order.

There is also the illegal way. You heard me—illegal. I'm not condoning it; I'm simply, uh, mentioning it. It's something called Second Acting.

SHH!!! That's all I'm saying on the subject.

THE MAJESTIC THEATRE LIVES UP TO ITS NAME. IT'S BEEN THE HOME TO *THE PHANTOM OF THE OPERA*, THE LONGEST-RUNNING SHOW IN BROADWAY HISTORY.

CHAPTER FOUR

Give My Regards to Broadway

Waiting for the star to leave the theater can be disappointing, especially when some of them don't even leave through the stage door! Some use an alternative exit to avoid the crowds.

Websites

A good way to keep updated on what's happening on Broadway is to go to the various Websites dedicated to all things theater. It's also a good way to spend an hour screaming at your computer screen because for every fabulous piece of theater news and/or gossip, there will be numerous postings discussing what a "no talent" various Tony Award winners are, how WICKED is awful or brilliant, and why Broadway is dead/better than ever.

Here are the main Websites:

Playbill.com

Playbill has Broadway news updates all day long and some fun features. My favorite is Diva Talk. Andrew Gans devotes his column to stalwart ladies like Betty Buckley, Bernadette Peters Jennifer Holliday, and Patti LuPone. There are also new divas like Carolee Carmello, Eden Espinoza, and Sara Ramirez who get stage time in Gans' column. The column is taglined "news, views, and reviews" and, I might add, interviews. It's always fun to hear what these ladies have to say. For instance, an article about Sutton Foster featured a photograph of her in flapper costume with her leg fully turned out and extended above her head, followed by the quote: "I don't think of myself as a dancer."

Then who *would* you think of as a dancer???

The testosterone counterpoint to Diva Talk is Wayman Wong's "The Leading Men" column. Chock full of news on stars like Patrick Wilson, Adam Pascal, and Brian Stokes Mitchell, the column seems to have a bent toward men who are s-e-x-y. Though it officially is called "The Leading Men," the subheading should read "Leading, shmeading . . . just look cute enough to be in a Tiger Beat foldout." You'll go for the interviews, but you'll stay for the photos!

Broadway.com

You'll find a nice smattering of news, gossip, and reviews at Broadway.com. (P.S. Kudos to whoever bought the domain name! The early bird . . .) My favorite is the "Ask a Star" video. People write in questions to the star being featured, and then Broaday.com chooses the questions and videotapes the star answering them! On other Websites, when a star answers a question a fan poses, the answer will be printed and it's impossible to know if the star or their publicist answered it, or worse yet, their underpaid assistant who's a sophomore at the local community college. But when you can see a video of Sandra Bernhard answering your question with a slow "yesssssssss, baby," you know it's really her!

BroadwayWorld.com

Then there's Broadwayworld.com. It's an excellent place to start because every day it compiles articles about Broadway from all other Websites and media sources. So instead of checking every Website, you can use Broadwayworld like a clearinghouse. Plus, it also features Broadwayworld radio where they play a ton of show tunes all day long. And not just your typical SOUTH PACIFIC chestnuts, but fun and obscure songs that will make you want to run out and buy the CD (SNOOPY: THE MUSICAL . . . the London version) or quickly lower the volume on your computer (Lauren Bacall singing . . . anything). But either way, you'll learn some new songs!

TalkinBroadway.com

As discussed in Chapter Three, TalkinBroadway.com has Shoppin' Broadway, which lists Broadway tickets people are selling. TalkinBroadway also has a guide to every show's policy for standing room tush tickets. The best reason to go, though, is their message board called All That Chat. Everybody, and I mean EVERYBODY, reads it, from the theater fan living in the boondocks to the top Broadway producers and actors. Though some actors have had to stop reading it because of the mean things people have posted about them (my Broadway pal calls it "the Devil's tool," and I know another Broadway diva who had to block it on her computer so she wouldn't be tempted to read it lest it devastate her). It has the *latest* news, gossip, gushings, and completely unconfirmed and unsubstantiated rumors. The people on the board are fiercely opinionated, and it's fun to read the kookiness that a disparaging remark about the bus-and-truck tour of Andrew Lloyd Webber's ASPECTS OF LOVE can bring. Here's a typical sampling:

This initial post was responding to the casting of Alexander Gemignani (who was then playing the Beadle in SWEENEY TODD) as Jean Valjean in the revival of LES MIZ.

Posted by NAME WITHELD
Subject: re: ...and Jean Valjean will be
Will they be lowering the score for him (as has been done in *Sweeney*)?

Posted by OTHER NAME WITHELD
Subject: First of all, "uninformed one" . . .
the Beadle music in the revival was lowered not because he doesn't have the notes... he does and then some. It was lowered because Sondheim wanted it so. In this production it needed to be more of a conversational sound, not some showy "listen to my high notes" sound. When YOU compose an award-winning musical, you can make the rules, too! Until then, don't assume so much. ps happy Mother's Day!
(Author comment: Note the PS . . . hilarious!)

Posted by: NAME WITHELD
Subject: re: First of all, "uninformed one"
My question was simply a question - not an attack of any kind. All I knew is that the score was lowered - there is no need to attack me and be so snide and condescending. God, I hate this board sometimes.
(Author's note: God, I love these boards *all* the time!!!!)

How To Be A Stargazer!

One of the best things about being in New York is the ample opportunity for celebrity spotting. And, unlike most you'll run into in L.A., these celebrities are famous because of actual talent, not because they went to third base with their best friend's ex-boyfriend (*Laguna Beach*, anyone?). But the question remains, how do you see a Broadway star aside from being in the audience? It's like bird watching: Find out where they usually congregate and plant yourself there. And be sure you're always armed with a digital camera, something to write on (a *Playbill*, a CD, this book, etc.) and a Sharpie. There's nothing worse than seeing your favorite star and neither of you having a writing implement. And, take it from me, eyeliner does not make an attractive autograph. (Especially if it's blue. I'm talking to you, Midwesterners!)

The Stage Door

Yes, we all know the scene after the curtain comes down at a hit Broadway show. An ungainly mob crowds outside the stage door to catch a glimpse of the star leaving. Unless you're in the front, it's often impossible to even see over the heads of the hoi polloi to catch a glimpse of the celeb milling through the crowd, let alone get an autograph, lock eyes with said celebrity, exchange numbers, and go on a date. Waiting for the star to leave the theater can be disappointing, especially when some of them don't even leave through the stage door! Some use an alternative exit to avoid the crowds.

How dare they not want to be mobbed and pawed!

The trick is to do the reverse of what the crowds do. Plant yourself at the stage door *before* the show! Everybody in a Broadway show has to arrive at the theater at some point. (Note: There is only one instance I know of that someone in a Broadway show was homeless and actually lived in his dressing room. It was due to a drug issue, but now he's clean and sober and has fantastic stories to tell!) The time every actor has to be in the theater is a half hour before the performance (known in show-biz lingo as "half hour"). Some people arrive at the theater way before that (Bernadette Peters always got to GYPSY two-and-a-half hours before the curtain), but if you're at the stage door an hour before the show, you're bound to see plenty of star wattage and a plethora of cute chorus boys and sexy chorines. Also, they won't be exhausted like after the show (and in a rush to get home), so you have a better chance of getting an autograph. Remember this old sailor's adage:

> *After a show,*
> *chances are low;*
> *before curtain,*
> *autograph certain!*

The Subway

While it's life altering for most of us to see an actual Broadway star up close, the ultimate Broadway fan loves *everybody* who trods those boards, lead and chorus dancer alike. Here's how to casually run into Broadway gypsies.

Most Broadway stars are provided a car in their contract to take them to and from the theater. But the gypsies take good old public transportation, so by positioning yourself in the right place at the right time, you're sure to get your share of grease-painted faces. The two main train subway stops used most frequently are Forty-second Street and Fiftieth Street because most Broadway theaters are from Fortieth to Fifty-fourth Street. If you just want to see a plethora of gypsies, go to the Times Square station on the corner of Broadway and Forty-second Street. Go down the stairs and through the turnstiles, and stand between the two staircases that lead to the downtown or uptown 1/2/3 trains. Get there Tuesday thru Saturday at 10:30 p.m., and you'll see a ton of Broadway folk till around 11:15. If you're waiting for a group of Broadway babies from a particular Broadway show, investigate how long and where the show is. For instance, if you love AVENUE Q, getting to the subway at 10:30 is too late because the show is only two hours, and most of the cast will have boarded trains by 10:30. Similarly, if you love the sassy singers in THE COLOR PURPLE, you should look for them at the Fiftieth Street station, since their theater is on Fifty-third Street and most aren't going to walk down to Forty-second. One of the advantages of this method is that after a show, Broadway folk are going somewhere (home) and before the show as well (the show!), but in the subway they have to wait for the train like the rest of us. If you see someone you want to meet, you can stand with them waiting for the train, perhaps strike up a conversation, and continue it as you ride the train! Yes! You're allowed to get on the same train they do, that's why it's called public transportation. But please take the hint and walk away if they obviously don't want to talk. For instance, while you're chatting them up, if they suddenly realize they have to make an important cell phone call, it's time to ixnay. Cell phones don't work in the subway. The frantic "Pardon me while I use my phone" is essentially the Broadway version of the "I think I hear my mother calling me."

Dance Class

There are two main dance studios in New York: Broadway Dance Center (usually called BDC, since everything on Broadway is abbreviated) and Steps. Both are great places for Broadway people spotting. Dancers often take class to keep up their technique and to network. If you wander into these buildings, you'll see a lot of faces that are in *Playbill*s. There are many Broadway folk teaching or taking classes. Word is, Donna McKechnie is often seen at Steps (Seventy-fourth and Broadway) in a ballet class. Hmm . . . I'm sure it's not intimidating at all to be dancing next to Cassie. I still have a devastating memory of struggling into a split next to Charlotte D'Amboise during a class at Broadway Dance Center (Fifty-seventh Street, east of Broadway). I essentially felt like Miss Piggy getting her makeup done next to Tyra Banks.

You'll also see plenty of ensemble members taking their daily class. Now, if you're too cheap and/or not a dancer and/or too intimidated to take a class, you can simply show up and stand around the front desk perusing the schedule while scoping the room. You're sure to see plenty of working gypsies and celebs trotting in and out. But the key is to go during the day. At night, the Broadway folk you want to see are on Broadway!

Theater District Restaurants

When you're on safari and you want to see the rhino or water buffalo, you go to their watering holes. The same is true on Broadway. Go to the watering holes (i.e., restaurants or bars) where actors are known to congregate. A good time to go is after a matinee on a

Wednesday or a Saturday. Many actors stay near the theater between shows because they don't want to travel home just to come back again. While some simply stay in the theater and take a nap, others eat in the theater district. NOT in one of the headache-y restaurants that tourists frequent thinking they're having a "real New York experience." Here's a rule: If the words "Hard Rock" or "Hollywood" are in the title, Broadway folk aren't the patrons. Go to Ollies on Forty-fourth Street right off Broadway. Delicious Chinese food and gypsies everywhere. Or Kodama on Forty-fifth Street and Eighth Avenue. Sushi and Equity members. Ninth Avenue also has a slew of great but moderately priced restaurants where you're sure to see gaggles of girls in sunglasses and hats. That outfit is a sure bet you're looking at a working actress. Most women don't want to reapply their false eyelashes once the eyelashes have been applied for the first show, so they keep them on all day. But these women also know that they look crazy walking around done up like a Vegas call girl, so they hide their hooker eyes with enormous sunglasses. Also, many women are wigged in Broadway shows and have to pin up their real hair and put it under a wig cap. They don't feel like undoing it and then washing and styling it, so they hide their wig caps under a stylish hat. I put the word "stylish" in there to make them feel better.

If you're looking for some gay guy you spotted in a show and thought was cute, stop by the bar called Therapy on Fifty-second between Eighth and Ninth Avenues after the show. You'll see many of the Broadway gay crowd. But remember, many Broadway folk are dancers, so be prepared to compare your abs to theirs and cry silent tears.

See also the special events listed in Chapter Six. Any of these will give you plenty of stars to gape at.

When you see someone you want to ask for an autograph, don't be shy. Most Broadway people like being recognized. Just make sure you know who the star is whom you are asking for an autograph. Telling Bea Arthur that she was wonderful in TORCH SONG TRILOGY (that was Harvey Fierstein) will get you one of her signature "St. Olaf" glares.

KNOW YOUR CLASSIC MUSICALS

1. What composer/lyricist team wrote "With a Little Bit of Luck" and "I Loved You Once in Silence"?

   a. *Rodgers and Hart*
   b. *Rodgers and Hammerstein*
   c. *Lerner and Lowe*
   d. *The Gershwins*

2. Who replaced Celeste Holm as Ado Annie in OKLAHOMA!?

   a. *Liz Taylor*
   b. *Shelly Winters*
   c. *Shirley MacLaine*
   d. *Dakota Fanning*

3. What show did Ethel Merman *not* star in?

   a. *Gypsy*
   b. *Hello, Dolly!*
   c. *Sound of Music*
   d. *Call Me Madam*

KNOW YOUR CLASSIC MUSICALS

4. In the Broadway show, ON THE TOWN, the woman who played the role of the lady taxi driver became a fixture on TV as the mother of whom?

   a. Shirley Feeney
   b. Laverne DeFazio
   c. Mary Richards
   d. Rhoda Morgenstern

5. Who was the star of both THE PAJAMA GAME and CAROUSEL?

   a. Gordon MacRae
   b. John Raitt
   c. Richard Kiley
   d. Little Richard

TALK ABOUT A GOOD-LUCK HOUSE FOR THE TONY AWARDS.
THE ST. JAMES HOSTS MEL BROOKS' *THE PRODUCERS*, WINNER
OF MORE TONYS THAN ANY OTHER SHOW IN THE HISTORY OF
BROADWAY.

CHAPTER FIVE

The Tony Awards (Scandals, Facts, and Dish)

The actual voting is done by around 750 theater professionals who must see every Broadway show, or at least not vote in a category in which they haven't seen every nominated performance. Unfortunately, there's no way to prove this.

THEATER FOLK, not unlike the film industry, love to laud themselves. There are the Drama Desk Awards, the Outer Critics Circle Awards, The Drama League Awards, and many online audience awards. However, we all know what really counts: The *Playbill* Leading

Man Award (mentioned only because I was one of the winners in 2003). And barring that, the Tony Award. Here is a guide to the mother of all theater awards.

Titled after the sassy nickname of Antoinette Perry, who was the wartime leader of the American Theatre Wing, the Tonys began in 1947. Back then, they were a much smaller affair, simply a dinner and awards ceremony that took place in the Grand Ballroom of the Waldorf-Astoria hotel. In 1967 they began to be televised, and theater fans across the country were able to see real Broadway performances broadcast into their living rooms. Many a young person's first exposure to musical theater happened while flipping through channels and landing on CBS one Sunday in June. In 1997, the Tonys broadcast moved from a Broadway theater to the enormous Radio City Music Hall (six thousand seats). This made it possible for the public to get seats. If you're interested in buying tickets to the Tonys, go to tonyawards.com for info. It's very exciting to see it live in the theater. Not only are you seeing what's being broadcast, but the commercial breaks feature live entertainment the viewers at home don't get to see! Often, the host will come out and kibbutz with the audience. Plus you can stand up during the breaks, whip out your opera glasses, and watch some diva reapply her lipstick or some Broadway hunk wipe the grease from his T-zone.

The nominating committee, made up of thirty theater professionals (agents, actors, scenic designers, etc.), see every Broadway show and vote by secret ballot. The nominations are usually what people expect, with one or two surprises thrown in every year. There have

only been a few actual scandals. One involved VICTOR/
VICTORIA. It was the big musical of the 1995–96 season
with elaborate sets, showy costumes, and big dance
numbers. Yet it garnered only one nomination. Julie
Andrews was nominated for best actress, overlooking
leading actor Tony Roberts and a brilliant performance
by Rachel York in the part Lesley Ann Warren played in
the film. Director Blake Edwards, choreographer Rob
Marshall (who later went on to direct/choreograph the
film version of CHICAGO), and the show itself were
also not nominated. Essentially, if you had anything
to do with VICTOR/VICTORIA and your name wasn't
Julie Andrews, you weren't nominated.

This precipitated the first snubbing of a nomination
and here's how it went down.

Julie Andrews publicly declined the nomination
because of how the rest of the production was
"egregiously" overlooked. The Tony committee had
no rules in place for a nomination decline and decided
to keep her name on the ballot, but voters knew she
had opted out. That year the Tony Award went to
Donna Murphy for THE KING AND I. Would Donna
have won if Julie had embraced her nomination? Who
knows? It's one of the many unsolved mysteries of that
soprano wrapped in an enigma who goes by the name
of Julie Andrews.

All right, back to how it works. The actual voting
is done by around seven hundred fifty theater professionals who must see every Broadway show, or at least
promise to not vote in a category in which they haven't
seen every nominated performance. Unfortunately,
there's no way to prove this. For instance, Doug Sills

gave a brilliant performance in THE SCARLET PIM-
PERNEL but lost the Tony Award to Alan Cumming in
CABARET. A source told me that allegedly many voters
never saw PIMPERNEL because even though Doug got
great reviews, the show didn't. Unfortunately, they still
voted in the best actor category. Would Alan have won
the Tony Award if every voter had seen THE SCARLET
PIMPERNEL? Who knows? It's one of the many unsolved mysteries of that emcee wrapped in an enigma
who goes by the name of Alan Cumming.

Another scandal happened in 2002. Not with the
nominations, but with the actual winner of best musical!
A lot of the Tony voters are people who have a stake in
theaters around the country. Therefore, they will benefit
if a Broadway show has a successful national tour.
Theater wags use that fact to explain the reason why
the show URINETOWN won the Tony Award for best
score, best book, *and* best Direction but lost the best
musical nod to THOROUGHLY MODERN MILLIE. The
Tony for best musical is MILLIE, but another musical
has the best book/score and Direction? Hmmm . . .

Most insiders think that the voters who had a stake in
national touring theaters felt THOROUGHLY MODERN
MILLIE would tour better than URINETOWN because
MILLIE has marquee recognition owing to it having
first been a film in the 1960s. Conversely, they felt that
bodily fluids don't go over well in the Midwest. The
thinking is that voters gave the Tony nod to MILLIE
to ensure a strong national tour and money in their
pockets. I'm not saying it's true; I'm just telling you
what the buzz was.

Two years later, it was WICKED versus AVENUE Q.

Insiders were saying AVENUE Q wouldn't tour well because it's a show with a small cast (ticket buyers usually want to spend money on a big spectacle) and it has dirty language and a graphic puppet-on-puppet sex scene (which is hilarious, but as usual, conservative states would frown upon it). The AVENUE Q producers thought that they were the critical favorite but were going to lose because voters who had touring theater connections would want to support the show they felt would have a more profitable national tour (i.e., WICKED)

Well, borrowing a page from the Harvey Weinstein school of Oscar campaigning, the AVENUE Q cast recorded a special song called "Rod's Dilemma" about the character Rod not knowing who to vote for in his upcoming Rotary Club election. He owed a favor to one candidate, thought another one was cute, but felt the third would do the best job. The other characters in the show sang a fun song imploring him to "vote his heart." The not-so-subtle message was vote for the show you think is best, not the show that will help you personally profit. The producers mailed the CD to every single Tony Award voter and on that fateful Sunday in 2004, AVENUE Q won best book, best score, *and* best musical. FYI, turns out WICKED didn't need the Tony anyway. They have an incredibly successful national tour and London company and continue to sell out on Broadway. So, Tony Shmony!

Notable Losses

Barbra Streisand did not win a Tony Award for her brilliant portrayal of Fanny Brice in FUNNY GIRL. That honor went to Carol Channing for her outstanding portrayal of Dolly Gallagher Levi in HELLO, DOLLY! Barbra got her comeuppance, though, when she snatched the role of Dolly away from Carol for the film version. Carol then got *her* comeuppance when the movie sucked!

Elaine Stritch, who is probably best known for her boozy and scathing portrayal of Joanne in COMPANY (where she originated her signature song "The Ladies Who Lunch"), *didn't* win the Tony Award for that performance! It actually went to Helen Gallagher for her wonderful, but nowadays mostly forgotten, performance in the revival of NO, NO, NANETTE.

A CHORUS LINE had many wonderful performances. Priscilla Lopez played the sweet and hopeful Morales (originating "Nothing" and "What I Did for Love") and Kelly Bishop played the sexy and acerbic Sheila who sings the section of "At the Ballet" about remembering her mother finding another woman's earrings in her father's car. The two actresses also shared a dressing room. They were both nominated for best featured actress in a musical and they were also best friends. Wouldn't it have been sweet if they had tied? They didn't. That year the Tony went to . . . Kelly Bishop. Priscilla said she was devastated that she didn't win but at the same time felt ecstatic for her friend. Don't cry for Priscilla, though. Four years later, she won the Tony for her hilarious portrayal of Harpo Marx in A DAY IN HOLLYWOOD/A NIGHT IN THE UKRAINE. Although to this day she is still devastated that when she won she was so overwhelmed, she forgot to thank Harpo during her speech.

Mortifying Gaffes

Elizabeth Taylor was asked to present at the Tony Awards, and as she held the list of nominations, she warned the audience that she has trouble reading (see any awards show with Elizabeth Taylor to know she was telling the truth). She then struggled through a list of producers, pronouncing the famous James Nederlander's name as "James Needle-heimer" getting an *enormous* laugh from the audience.

C'mon! Needle-heimer? As in "John Jacob Needle-heimer Schmidt"?

Ingrid Bergman read off the names of the best score nominees in the early seventies. When she got to Sondheim, she pronounced Stephen as *Stefan* in her Swedish accent. There was an awkward laugh in the audience. She then read the winner . . . and welcomed to the stage Stefan Sondheim. Hello!? Or should I say Hallá där? One of the greatest Broadway composers ever! I'm sure *he'd* know how to pronounce the famous Swedish composer Baron Anders von Düben. (Author's note: Thank you, Google)

Notable Wins

Daisy Egan is the youngest Tony Award winner. She played Mary Lennox in THE SECRET GARDEN and won for best featured actress at age 12. I'm sure her win was looked upon "fondly" by the older actresses in her category. Speaking of which, her closest contender in the category that year was LaChanze, who was nominated for ONCE ON THIS ISLAND. She wound up finally winning her first Tony Award . . . as best actress for THE COLOR PURPLE. But it took her fifteen years!

The most Tony Awards belong to Harold Prince (twenty-one awards), including eight for directing, eight for producing, two as producer of the year's best musical, and three special Tony Awards.

Stephen Sondheim is the composer who has the most Tony Awards. He's won seven, but only for six shows because the best score category used to be divided into best Music and best Lyrics. He won best score for PASSION, INTO THE WOODS, SWEENEY TODD, A LITTLE NIGHT MUSIC, and FOLLIES and best music and best lyrics for COMPANY.

The youngest actress with the most Tony Awards is Audra MacDonald who now has four Tonys (tying with Gwen Verdon, Angela Lansbury, and Zoe Caldwell). She won her first for playing Carrie in the revival of CAROUSEL (best featured actress in a musical). Her second was for a playing a nervous soprano who gets dished by Maria Callas and then dishes her right back in

MASTER CLASS (best featured actress in a play). Then came the role of the doomed Sarah in RAGTIME (best featured actress in a musical), and finally she won for playing opposite Sean "P Diddy" Combs in A RAISIN IN THE SUN (best featured actress in a play). She's still young enough that she can tie or out-win Julie Harris, the actress with the most Tony Awards (Julie Harris has won five times: I AM A CAMERA, THE LARK, FORTY CARATS, THE LAST OF MRS. LINCOLN, and THE BELLE OF AMHERST). FYI, I accompanied Audra at her senior recital from Juilliard. I have no (zero) Tony Awards.

Question: I want to see old Tony Award performances! What do I do?

Answer: The best thing is to buy the fabulous DVD *Broadway's Lost Treasures: The Best of the Tony Awards.* As of this writing, there are three discs available. They each consist of fantastic performances from past Tony Awards. First, note the length of time shows were allowed to perform before TV execs decided to allot each musical only three minutes. Back in the seventies, ANNIE did three complete songs! Maybe one day, the Tony producers will wise up and allow TV audiences across the country a big slice of Broadway instead of a paltry amuse-bouche.

If you have to choose which disc to get first, I would recommend purchasing them in order.

Volume One has incredible Diva performances: Dorothy Loudon as ANNIE'S Miss Hannigan, sassily pulsating her groin during "Easy Street," Betty Buckley's intense and chilling performance of "Memory" from

CATS, and Patti LuPone's star turn belting out EVITA's first-act finale, "A New Argentina."

Volume Two has some stand-out divo performances: Colm Wilkinson as LES MIZ's Jean Valjean joining in the rousing "One Day More." (Note: Watch the wonderful Frances Ruffele, who plays Eponine, get her lip stuck to Marius. Reminder to actors: Use Chapstick before a performance.)

Don't miss Jerry Orbach as Chicago's hottest lawyer, Billy Flynn (Note: Bebe Neuwirth has said he was the sexiest man she's ever seen on Broadway). You also get GRAND HOTEL's "Take a Glass Together," one of Tommy Tune's most brilliantly staged numbers. Michael Jeter appears to have legs made out of rubber, and watching him makes you understand why he won the Tony. I guarantee you'll be rewinding over and over again to watch this incredible performance.

This brings me to another question: *Why aren't Broadway shows videotaped????* They are! Or at least some are. And there are different ways for you to see them. There are some videos that are commercially available and can be bought at most video stores. Here are my top choices:

Filmed Performances

SUNDAY IN THE PARK WITH GEORGE with Mandy Patinkin and Bernadette Peters. Act Two is sort of a headache, but it won Stephen Sondheim a Pulitzer Prize and the two leads are Broadway royalty. Spot the little girl in the park. It's Danielle Ferland. A few years later she was Little Red Riding Hood in Sondheim's INTO THE WOODS.

PIPPIN starring Willian Katt ("The Greatest American Hero"! Anybody?). Stephen Schwartz (WICKED) wrote a brilliant score (when he was in his early twenties), and the Fosse choreography is still the definition of sexy. Plus it features Ben Vereen and Chita Rivera, two actual triple threats.

Filmed Performances Combined with Rehearsal Footage

FOLLIES in Concert. This was a concert version done at New York's Avery Fisher Hall in the mid-eighties with a brilliant cast. Barbara Cook is heartbreaking as Dorothy, the aging chorus girl who sings every codependent's anthem, "Losing My Mind," and Elaine Stritch brings the house down with her deadpan "Broadway Baby." Plus, since half the video is of rehearsals leading up to the big night, there's great footage of these Broadway greats learning dance steps and harmonies. Mandy Patinkin is shown as a slight nut job, Lee Remick is a nervous Nellie, and not surprisingly, Elaine Stritch is a cranky ass!

Speaking of Stritch, her one-woman show ELAINE STRITCH: AT LIBERTY is a must see. She tells tales out of school about Judy Garland, the bitchery of other famous actresses, and shows us what it was like for her to be a raging alcoholic (she's sober now) while simultaneously somehow giving brilliant performances onstage.

Broadway and Then Some

These are videos that don't fit into any category.

Broadway: The Golden Age contains in-depth interviews with almost every major star who performed during Broadway's golden age. Jerry Orbach, Gwen Verdon, Eli Wallach, Angela Lansbury, Bea Arthur, Ben Gazzara, etc . . . plus never-before-seen footage of classic shows and star performances (Angela Lansbury doing MAME, the original OKLAHOMA! in 1943). It's a great way to learn your who's who of theater and why the "Golden Age" got that name. (PS: Check out Edie Adam's eye makeup!)

COMPANY: This film documented the recording session of the 1970 Sondheim classic, COMPANY. First of all, the amount of people brazenly smoking in the recording studio is fascinating in itself. Also, just like looking at a car accident you can't turn away from, you'll love watching the section with Elaine Stritch struggling through "The Ladies Who Lunch." Here's what happened: To save money, albums are usually recorded all in one day, and by the time Stritch stepped up to the microphone, it was well past midnight and her voice was shot. No matter how much she tried (even dropping the key of the song a step lower), no one in the studio, including herself, was satisfied with her performance of the song. I'd tell you how it ends up, but I want you to watch the DVD!

Moon over Broadway: This is a scathing look at the nightmarish process of mounting the Broadway comedy MOON OVER BUFFALO starring Carol Burnett and Phillip Bosco. A documentary film crew recorded rehearsals, interviews, and the private creative meetings with the producers, writer, and director. The pressure of mounting a show that isn't going well is revealed in all its ugly glory. (Note: Carol Burnett comes out smelling like a rose!)

Seth's Broadway Chatterbox

Self-promoting? Oh, I couldn't. Since 1999, I've been
interviewing Broadway stars during my live talk show
in New York City. Past guests have included Matthew
Broderick, Megan Mullally, Idina Menzel, and Audra
MacDonald. They talk about their greatest triumphs,
biggest flops, and also bring in a mortifying video clip
from their past (sometimes a high school show, a soap
opera walk-on, or a devastatingly tacky theme-park
revue). Watch the clip of Kristin Chenoweth losing the
Miss Pennsylvania pageant, and you'll see bitchery at its
best! The Chatterbox usually culminates with the star
performing their signature song. There's a combo DVD
available of just the performances, including Kristin
Chenoweth singing "My Funny Valentine," Idina Menzel
singing "Life of the Party," and Betty Buckley singing
"Memory." All the money goes to BC/EFA. DVDs are
available at www.sethsbroadwaychatterbox.com.

Video taped performances can also be seen at:

THE MUSEUM OF TELEVISION & RADIO, which has twenty-
five thousand tapes of radio and TV broadcasts,
including some fabulous Broadway shows that
were filmed for TV! See the hilarious Roz Russell in
WONDERFUL TOWN. See pre–*Victor/Victoria* Lesley
Ann Warren in the TV version of CINDERELLA.
The museum is at 25 West Fifty-second Street, just
off Sixth Avenue. It's open Wednesdays through
Saturdays from noon to five and Tuesdays noon to
eight. Suggested contribution is $3, $1.50 for children
under 13. For information, call (212) 621-6800.

**THE NEW YORK PUBLIC LIBRARY FOR THE PERFORMING
ARTS.** For around twenty years, almost every

Broadway show has been filmed for the archives at this library located in Lincoln Center. It's thrilling to see actual performances of Broadway shows . . . especially those that didn't stay around for long. See the short-lived but musically brilliant CHESS. See gymnast Kathy Rigby in SEUSSICAL as the third Cat in the Hat (number one was David Shiner, who mysteriously left a few weeks after opening, and number two was Rosie O'Donnell who played it for a month while doing her talk show during the day).

Illegal Bootlegs

There is a whole underground network of videos that were taped illegally from the audience. Many actors, stagehands, musicians, etc. are anti-bootlegs. Others tacitly accept that they exist, and still others are thrilled to get copies of their performances that they can keep for posterity. I myself have no problem with them as long as the person selling them isn't making a profit off other people's work. If you're interested, simply post a request with your email on one of the many theater boards. The post will be removed due to its illegal nature, but someone will probably respond before that happens. Trading them is my preferred method of bootleg commerce . . . if indeed I had any . . . which I don't (if anybody from the unions are reading this).

Ah! Excellent cover-up, Seth!

THE NEWLY-RENAMED AUGUST WILSON THEATRE, WHERE THE
RED-HOT SMASH *JERSEY BOYS* SEEMS SETTLED FOR A LONG
RUN. THE THEATRE HAS ALSO GONE BY THE NAMES THE ANTA
AND THE VIRGINIA.

CHAPTER SIX

Broadway's Special Events

Q FACT

You will see the likes of Bernadette Peters, Julia Roberts, and Mary Tyler Moore, and you have a one in two chance of sitting next to a hot chorus guy or girl in the audience.

THE FIRST preview of a Broadway show is full of mystery. The cast doesn't know what to expect. Will the audience love it? Or will there be a ton of empty seats after intermission? Will they laugh at all the jokes? Or laugh at the leading lady's thinly disguised weight gain?

Likewise, the audience doesn't know what to expect. There hasn't been much buzz about the show, good or bad, because no one has yet to see it. This tension adds an incredibly level of excitement to the evening. There is that same excitement during the many special events Broadway has each year. Because they're only one or two nights, they have that "first preview" thrill. If you're in New York during any of these events, buy a ticket and be an insider!

Gypsy of the Year / The Easter Bonnet Competition

Twice a year, for six weeks, Broadway shows raise money for Broadway Cares/Equity Fights Aids. They usually do a curtain speech asking for donations and offer things like autographed posters/*Playbill*s or photos with the leads. Some shows offer more creative things, like Harvey Fierstein leaving an outgoing message on your answering machine (HAIRSPRAY) or a backstage tea party with Chita Rivera (THE DANCER'S LIFE) or one night of lovemaking with Hugh Jackman (this is something I pitched to Mr. Jackman . . . still awaiting a response). To celebrate each fundraising period, the productions that participate put on a big, fat variety show. In the fall, it's the GYPSY OF THE YEAR COMPETITION and the spring has THE EASTER BONNET COMPETITION. The shows consist of comedy sketches, big production numbers, and elaborate dances. It is Broadway at its best. First of all, it's totally star studded, Onstage and in the audience. You will see the likes of Bernadette Peters, Julia Roberts, and Mary Tyler Moore, and you have a one in two chance of sitting next to a hot chorus guy or girl in the audience (note: bring plenty of cards with your phone number for "working it"). Sometimes the sketches are extremely moving (the LION KING had two beautiful male dancers doing an athletic, sensuous dance while a recording played of real-life interviews with men talking about their experiences growing up gay). Sometimes they're hilarious (FIDDLER ON THE ROOF teamed up with AVENUE Q to form AVENUE JEW ... they won the competition that year!). The show itself is open to the public, but you'll feel like a true insider if you buy a ticket. If you can't attend, you can actually buy a DVD – and it's not illegal! GYPSY OF THE YEAR and EASTER BONNET are filmed each year, and the money from the sale of the DVDs goes to BC/EFA. You'll be the envy of your friends when you own a clip of Glenn Close hilariously recreating her *Fatal Attraction* character (1994 EASTER BONNET) or Idina Menzel belting out the finale song two months before she won the Tony Award (2004 EASTER BONNET). Go to www.Broadwaybeat.com to purchase!

The Broadway Flea Market

This event is held every fall in Shubert Alley and sponsored by BC/EFA. Broadway casts set up booths where they sell posters and tons of memorabilia from their shows. They also sell delicious treats and lots of other stuff. A big auction takes place in the center of Shubert Alley, where fantastic stuff is given to the highest bidder. Luxury trips, tours of your favorite TV shows, meals with celebs, and much more! There's also a line where you can pay a small admission fee and walk down a slew of tables for autographs from a gazillion celebrities. There is a new batch that comes in every hour, so you're bound to see your favorite star if you're willing to wait.

Broadway Barks

This is also held in Shubert Alley and features animal-loving celebrities. It's hosted by Mary Tyler Moore and Bernadette Peters, and if you show up, you'll see both of these ladies, plus tons of Broadway stars. The event supports numerous animal shelters, and there is always a plethora of cute cats and adorable dogs to adopt.

Broadway Bares

During THE WILL ROGERS FOLLIES Broadway director/choreographer Jerry Mitchell was then a featured dancer who bared his butt eight times a week in one of the numbers. It gave him the idea to put on a tasteful but sexy strip show with other Broadway dancers at Splash, a sassy gay bar in New York's Chelsea neighborhood. Those hot Broadway bitches shook it on the bar and raised eight thousand dollars that night in 1991. It's now expanded to a fully staged, sold-out extravaganza featuring a calvacade of hotties (both male and female) from the Great White Way. In 2006, it raised $659,500! The show always has a theme, and the strips are choreographed around that theme. During the superhero year, who can forget SPAMALOT star Chris Sieber as Batman with his real-life gypsy boyfriend, Kevin Burrows, dressed as Robin? Since I was a child, I'd been hoping to see the dynamic duo make out and now I own that make-out session on DVD! That's right, if you can't make the event, you can buy it so you can watch it (and rewatch it and pause it) in the privacy of your home (at www.broadwaybeat.com).

Nothin' Like A Dame

The Broadway diva is a staple of the gay man's brunch conversation. Who can't spend hours debating Patti LuPone's Evita versus Betty Buckley's Grizabella? And don't even get me started on Idina Menzel's Elphaba versus Heather Headley's Aida if you don't have at least an hour to spare. My point is that once a year there is an extravaganza called NOTHIN' LIKE A DAME featuring divas (Bernadette Peters), divas in training (Eden Espinoza), and pathetic, wannabe divas (me, in the audience). This estrogen fest was started to help the Phyllis Newman Women's Health Initiative, which helps Broadway ladies with breast and ovarian cancer and other female-related illnesses. Broadway's brassiest leading ladies get together for one night only of music and comedy. In one show, Rosie did a stand-up routine that included a section about Star Jones's miraculous one-hundred-pound-plus weight loss that Star attributed to only Pilates. Suffice it to say, if Star had been there she would have laughed hard enough to split her stomach staples . . . I mean her Pilates. You can see the event live, or go to broadwaybeat.com to own your own DVD.

Joe's Pub / Ars Nova

There are many great cabaret spaces in New York, but Broadway folk tend to perform at two spaces. The first is part of The Public Theater, which opened a cabaret space in 2002 and named it Joe's Pub, after the Public's founder, Joseph Papp. Ars Nova opened in 2000 and was founded by Jon Steingart and his wife Jenny Weiner in memory of her brother, Gabe. They both always have some fabulous Broadway person strutting their stuff. Melba Moore, Cheyenne Jackson, and Audra MacDonald have all appeared at Joe's Pub, while Ars Nova has a more hot-and-upcoming crowd like Manoel Felciano (SWEENEY TODD), Daniel Reichard (JERSEY BOYS), and Lisa Howard (THE 25TH ANNUAL PUTNAM COUNTY SPELLING BEE). Go to their Websites (arsnovanyc.com or joespub.com) and see who's performing next. It's always cool to see a Broadway performer out of a Broadway show doing the music they love to sing. It's also fun to see who's in the audience. Stephen Sondheim's been known to show up at Ars Nova and I'm sure would welcome your chattering for the full fifteen minutes before the show begins.

"So . . . Mr. Sondheim? Can I call you Steve? Anyhoo . . . which comes first? The music or the lyrics? Wait, before you answer . . . was Jack Gilford a bitch? Because . . . where are you going? The show hasn't begun . . . .Mr. Sondheim? Steve? Stefan??!!!"

Encores

The Encores Series started in 1994 and takes place at Midtown's City Center. It's a series of three shows done in concert versions, meaning the actors hold their scripts and the orchestra is onstage. But there are still choreographed numbers, and because the show's not polished, it gives the audience an intimacy they don't from a typical Broadway show. The series began to highlight obscure musicals (ALLEGRO, BLOOMER GIRL) but there's always at least one well-known show done each season (BYE BYE BIRDIE, CAN CAN). Encores casts the biggest Broadway stars around (Bebe Neuwirth, Martin Short, Victor Garber), rehearses them for one week, and shoves them in front of an audience. There are always flubbed lines and missed cues, but you feel like a total insider watching it unfold. Two of the Encore's concerts made it to Broadway: the Tony-nominated WONDERFUL TOWN with Donna Murphy and the long-running hit, CHICAGO. Without Encores reviving interest in CHICAGO, it never would have been made into a movie, and the new movie-musical craze (THE PRODUCERS, RENT, HAIRSPRAY) never would have happened. Go to www.nycitycenter. org for details.

The Actors' Fund Annual Fall Concert

In 2001 an incredibly handsome man came up with the idea of doing a concert version of DREAMGIRLS. That man . . . was me! I had always been obsessed with DREAMGIRLS, and one year I was doing a benefit for Beth Simchat Torah, New York's lesbian and gay synagogue. I did a number from the show, and Lillias White sang the role of Effie. There's video footage of that performance, and you see me leap up from the piano in the middle of the number because I was so blown away by Lillias belting a high G with vibrato! I immediately decided I had to conduct DREAMGIRLS one day with a full orchestra, with Lillias as Effie. I approached the Actors' Fund and they loved the idea. I suggested Audra MacDonald, who had just won her third Tony Award, as Deena because I knew she had always coveted the role, and they suggested Heather Headley as Lorrell because she was super hot, having just received the Tony Award for AIDA. I called the composer, Henry Kreiger, who gave the concert his blessing, and we put the tickets on sale. Suffice it to say, we sold out and raised almost one million dollars for the Actors' Fund! We also wound up getting a record deal and recorded the whole concert! This began the Actors' Fund Concert Series, which takes place every fall. The second show we did was FUNNY GIRL, which I used as an opportunity for women who would be great as fanny Brice but probably wouldn't ever be cast, such as Whoopi Goldberg and Sutton Foster. Each diva played Fanny for one scene/song, and eventually the cast grew to include Idina Menzel, Judy Kuhn, and Ana Gasteyer. The following year was CHESS starring the brilliant belt-ress Julia Murney and International Man of Song, Josh Groban. The fourth concert was the first Broadway show I ever saw . . . HAIR. I went back to my concept for FUNNY GIRL and had a different Broadway star per number. We had Adam Pascal, Lea DeLaria, Raul Esparza, and *many* others. We wound up getting a recording deal for HAIR, and the CD was nominated for a Grammy Award! In 2005 we did ON THE TWENTIETH CENTURY, with the comic stylings of Marin Mazzie, Doug Sills, and *Laugh-In*'s Joanne Worley! Check out www.actorsfund.org for the next concert, and come and support a worthy cause!

There's a whole underworld to Broadway with fabulous events you can't even imagine, so it's best to check out the theater Websites to see what's coming up.

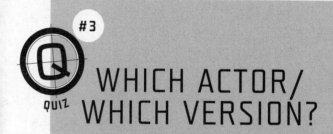

#3

WHICH ACTOR/ WHICH VERSION?

QUIZ

1. Name the actresses who played Maria in the Broadway and movie versions of WEST SIDE STORY.

2. Name the three actresses who played Velma Kelly in the original, revival, and film versions of CHICAGO.

3. Name the Edna Turnblad's from the original film, Broadway musical, and musical film of HAIRSPRAY.

4. Name the actresses who played Mimi in the Broadway and film versions of RENT.

5. Name the actresses who played Mama Rose in the original Broadway show, the film, the London production in the seventies, the eighties revival, the nineties TV version, and the 2003 revival.

45TH STREET BETWEEN BROADWAY AND EIGHTH IS A HOTBED OF BROADWAY THEATRES, INCLUDING THE ALWAYS-POPULAR HOUSE, THE GERALD SCHOENFELD THEATRE (FORMERLY THE PLYMOUTH).

CHAPTER SEVEN

Top 10 Broadway CDs You Must Have (and One Off-Broadway)

FACT

Usually, an overture is an imposition you have to sit through while you impatiently wait for the first song. This overture is a destination.

1. West Side Story

WHICH VERSION: The original Broadway.

BACKGROUND: Based on ROMEO AND JULIET, it was originally going to be called "East Side Story" and focus on a Jewish/Christian romance. To make it more relevant to the time (the 1950s), the plot was changed to focus on juvenile delinquency and the rivalry between American and Puerto Rican gangs. Shockingly, the show didn't get great reviews. It lost the Tony Award to THE MUSIC MAN and didn't become the phenomenon we know it as until the movie became a hit.

GAY ASPECT: Created by Sondheim, Leonard Bernstein, Arthur Laurents, and Jerome Robbins, it's a Fire Island summer share of geniuses. Also, cute (and gay!) Larry Kert is Tony, the star-crossed lover, and diva Chita Rivera is the sassy Anita.

BEST SONGS: *America:* The Sondheim lyrics are rapid fire and full of jokes, even if a lot of them go by too fast to understand. And listen to Chita's old-school, no-microphone belting! Remember, she had to sing this whole song and dance up a storm at the same time. Also, marvel at the instrumental sections. Normally, the music during a dance break in a Broadway song consists of the main melody reworked in a creative way. Leonard Bernstein, however, composed his dance breaks like symphonic works. They're not just the main music themes of "America" cobbled together by a dance arranger, they're totally different melodically and could stand alone as an orchestral work. Listen especially to the ending music as it builds, and don't resist the urge to shout out "olé" with Chita. Do resist the urge to put on those "F--- me" shoes the Shark Girls wear. They're bad for your ankles.

The Tonight Quintet: Listen to the cool opening fanfare chords over the ominous bass, and you'll hear why Bernstein was considered a master. This song is written in that musical theater form where every character has their own special solo section, and then they all sing together at the end. Note how everybody onstage sounds excited and happy, but the orchestra underneath is tense and foreboding.

That's because every character is setting up his or her doom. The Sharks and the Jets are psyched about their upcoming rumble, not knowing that one member of each gang will wind up dead. Tony is convinced by Riff to join in the rumble that will end with Riff being killed and Tony knifing the murderer. Maria is anxious for "tonight," when she'll meet up with Tony . . . not knowing that by the end of it he will have murdered her brother, Bernardo. Anita is singing about how aroused she'll be when she sees Bernardo later on, not knowing that she'll never see Bernardo again. The climax is thrilling. There's nothing more thrilling than a full Broadway chorus hitting a big, fat chord, with a soprano on the high C.

TIDBIT TO NAME-DROP TO YOUR FRIENDS: The show was directed by the infamous Robbins. A brilliant director whom some loved but many thought was too harsh to his actors, Broadway folklore states that one day Robbins was reaming his cast while standing perilously close to the orchestra pit. As he told them off, he kept moving backwards and nobody in the cast called out a warning until he finally fell into the pit!

2. A Chorus Line

WHICH VERSION: NOT THE MOVIE!!!!!!

BACKGROUND: The original show was groundbreaking on many levels. It was the first developed from a "workshop." In those days, most shows would go out of town to work out their kinks and then come to Broadway. This show was "workshopped" in New York (a few weeks rehearsal and then a presentation), which is the way most shows are developed nowadays. Michael Bennett created this method, and Joe Papp at the Public Theater green-lighted it. Real-life Broadway dancers co-created A CHORUS LINE. They all met at midnight after their shows, took a dance class, and then sat around in a circle talking about all their experiences with dancing. These sessions were tape-recorded and then dramatized and/or musicalized for the show. No one suspected the show would be a mega-hit. As a matter of fact, the first version ran for four hours!!! But according to the composer Marvin Hamlisch, Michael Bennett was a genius at knowing what to cut. Not enormous sections, but a line here, a song verse there, ultimately whittling the behemoth down to two hours. When the show was finally in shape, it opened off-Broadway at the Public Theater and became the hottest ticket in town. It then transferred to Broadway and won many Tony Awards *and* the Pulitzer Prize. It also became the longest-running musical, but that honor was usurped first by CATS and then THE PHANTOM OF THE OPERA. I guess there are worse things in the world to be devastated about … but I can't think of any.

GAY ASPECT: Paul, the first well-formed gay character in a musical, was played by Sammy Williams, who won a Tony Award for best featured actor in a Broadway musical.

BEST SONGS: *At the Ballet:* "At the Ballet" was based on the tape-recorded stories of Kelly Bishop (Sheila) and Nancy Lane (Bebe). Maggie's verse about an Indian chief asking her to dance is actually Donna McKechnie's story. Listen to how all parts about the painful childhoods are in a minor key (Sheila sings about her parents unhappy marriage, Bebe sings about realizing that she'd never be beautiful), but when they sing about everything being beautiful at the ballet, it goes into a soaring melody in a major key.

This song resonates for so many artists, and especially the queer community because every gay kid can identify with needing a place to escape to when we were children. The most exciting musical part is when Maggie builds her phrase and ends holding the last note of the word " bal-la-a-a-a-a-a-a-a-ay!!!!" That bee-atch is hitting a high E!

Nothing: Priscilla Lopez really did go to the High School of Performing Arts, and everything in the song really happened. Listen how well the lyricist, Ed Kleban, changes the meaning of the word "nothing" from something negative in her life to something positive. (She feels belittled by her teacher because she feels "nothing" during an improv but then realizes the course and the teacher himself are "nothing.")

Like I said, everything that's mentioned in the song really happened, but what isn't revealed in the song is the way Mr. Carp died: He committed suicide! The very next year he shot himself, and Priscilla Lopez sees that as proof that he had some major issues!

TIDBIT TO NAME-DROP TO YOUR FRIENDS: When A CHORUS LINE first opened off-Broadway, audiences definitely loved it, *but* the show wasn't getting a standing ovation. No one knew what to do. Finally, Marsha Mason came to see it and came backstage and told the creators she knew what the problem was: Cassie *had* to make the show. In the original version, Cassie auditions for the job, but the director can't bear the thought of a star dancer returning to the chorus and therefore doesn't cast her. Well, the audience loved Cassie so much they were devastated at the end of the show when she didn't get the gig. So, Michael Bennett changed the ending and Cassie got cast. As soon as that happened, the show got a standing ovation!

3. Evita

WHICH VERSION: Yet again, NOT THE MOVIE! No one has *ever* sung this score like Patti LuPone. When she first looked at the Lloyd Webber score with its nonstop belted high notes, it was rumored that she said "This man obviously *hates* women." She couldn't believe how difficult it was to sing. But that's not to say she couldn't do it . . . and brilliantly!!! As opposed to a certain pop star who took the songs down many a key … and still managed to give me a headache.

BACKGROUND: This was one of the first "sung thru" musicals, which then became very big in the eighties (CATS, LES MIZ, etc …) and the last collaboration between Tim Rice and Andrew Lloyd Webber (JESUS CHRIST SUPERSTAR, JOSEPH AND THE AMAZING TECHNICOLOR DREAMCOAT). The show started in London as a concept album with Julie Covington, opened on the West End with Elaine Paige, and took the Great White Way by storm, winning numerous Tony Awards including best musical and a best actress nod for Patti.

GAY ASPECT: Who hasn't dreamed of wearing that white dress and standing on that balcony?

BEST SONGS: *A New Argentina:* This is the song that the cast performed on the TONY awards which is available to watch on *Broadway's Lost Treasures*. The thing that makes this song spectacular is a phrase Patti sings three times. It features a string of super high notes that are belted. First, Patti sails through sixteen high E's. Then she sings it again with just as much power. Finally, she repeats the same phrase but, this time, instead of straights E's, she goes up to a high G!

That's one of the highest notes ever belted on Broadway! No wonder she only did six shows a week!!! (Terri Klausner did the Wednesday and Saturday matinees.)

"RAINBOW HIGH" This is the ultimate diva song. Evita is getting glammed out to go on a world tour, and she's surrounded by her beauty posse. The men sing of everything they're concentrating on to make her a superstar, chanting words like "eyes," "magic," and "diamonds." Three things I focus on every morning as I get dressed. Make sure you listen to Patti's fabulous voice every time she sings "rain-BOW hi-i-i-i-i-igh!" Thrilling! The most exciting part is when she modulates and sings the word "savior." Be sure to compare and contrast it to Madonna's version. Patti holds out the high note with fervor. Madonna holds it for one second and falls off it, giving the impression that she tripped over something in the recording studio and had no time to re-record it.

TIDBIT TO NAME-DROP TO YOUR FRIENDS: Nancy Opel was the understudy for Patti LuPone, and when she first went on, no one warned her about the cable that was stretched across the stage, which she was supposed to step over. So right after she sang "Don't Cry for Me, Argentina" in the beautiful while dress, she tripped over the cable, and went down flat on her back. Mandy Patinkin was onstage at the time singing a song about how beautiful Evita is while Nancy was awkwardly trying to get up. Because it was a hoop skirt, she had to roll to and fro on her back before she could get enough leverage to stand. So, the audience watched half the song with Mandy singing about how glamorous Evita was while she rolled around on her back like a cockroach with its legs in the air. When Nancy finally stood up, she decided to think fast and pretend that the mortifying fall was actually a foreshadowing of Evita's untimely death from ovarian cancer at the end of the show. So she stood up, clutched her uterine area, and grimaced. She laughs about it today, but also notes she never took over the role!

4. Gypsy

WHICH VERSION: Please, not the movie (Roz Russell just ain't a singer) and *not* the Tyne Daly version either. Neither holds a candle to the vocal chops of the Merm. GYPSY is the story of the ultimate stage mother, Mama Rose. It was the culmination of Ethel Merman's career gave birth to one of the most famous entrance lines: "Sing out, Louise!"

GAY ASPECT: Lyrics by Stephen Sondheim and book by Arthur Laurents. Gay + Gay = Gay!

BEST SONGS: *Overture:* Usually, an overture is an imposition you have to sit through while you impatiently wait for the first song. This overture is a destination. When you hear the opening trumpet "I Had a Dream" melody, through the brassy stripper section in the middle to the frantic violins at the end leading to last-held B-flat, you'll know why it's considered the best Broadway overture ever.

Everything's Coming Up Roses: Contrary to moronic beauty pageant contestants who sing this song with a plastic smile on their face (and Vaseline on their teeth), "Everything's Coming Up Roses" is anything but a positive, happy-go-lucky show tune. It's a devastating demonstration of steely denial. Rose's younger daughter, June, whom Rose has spent her life molding into a star, has run away with a dancer. Rose is left with Herbie, her boyfriend who wants to settle down and get married, and Louise, her other daughter, whom she's always treated as the untalented one. Both Herbie and Louise want to finally get out of the business, but Rose can't admit defeat. She also can't deal with her feelings about being abandoned by her youngest daughter, so she goes from a complete shutdown when she hears the news to a hyper happiness, during which she decides to focus all her energy on making Louise a star. All the cheer and joy in the lyrics are belied by the mania in Mama Rose's eyes and the looks of terror and sadness on the faces of Louise and Herbie. So when you listen to it, imagine the song in the context of the show, and it will take on a new meaning with multiple layers. And if you don't have the energy for all that, just listen to La Merman belt!

TIDBIT TO NAME-DROP TO YOUR FRIENDS: In the 1980s, Lauren Bacall was starring in WOMAN OF THE YEAR and had won her second Tony Award. No one really acknowledged out loud that when she sang, she sounded like a moose. Ethel Merman came to see the show and sat in the front of the theater. When Lauren walked out on stage at the beginning of the show and sang her first musical phrase in her signature baritone, Ethel recoiled and exclaimed, full volume, "Je-sus Kee-rist!!"

---

5. Hair

WHICH VERSION: The movie and the Broadway CDs are both great! They each have a different flavor. I also recommend the CD for the Actors' Fund that I music-directed featuring Jennifer Hudson, Adam Pascal, Lea DeLaria, and a ton of other Broadway stars!

BACKGROUND: HAIR was the first "rock musical," which was followed by hits like JESUS CHRIST SUPERSTAR and flops like DUDE and which laid the groundwork for the Pulitzer Prize–winning RENT. It started (like A CHORUS LINE) at the Public Theater and moved to Broadway in 1968. The show dealt with the growing unpopularity of the Vietnam War and had a decidedly antiwar sentiment. The music was as hip as what was being played on the radio instead of behind the times, which most of the sixties musicals were. Plus, there was a nude scene. Yes, a nude scene in a musical! This was *very* different than what was on Broadway at the time. Suffice it to say, in MAME Angela Lansbury and Bea Arthur didn't go the full monty. Because of the sex (there's a song called "Sodomy"), drugs (there's a song called "Hashish"), and rock-and-roll (the whole score!). HAIR was *the* show to see if you were young.

GAY ASPECT: Margaret Mead makes an appearance and tells the cast that they can be whatever they want, as long as they don't hurt anybody, which RuPaul once said was an inspiration for the way he lives his life.

BEST SONGS: *Frank Mills:* This song is basically a young girl asking if anyone has seen a boy she loves whose address she's lost. There is something so simple and plaintive about this song that when you listen to it, you'll immediately remember the innocence of when you first started dating. I've always been fascinated by the lyrics because they don't rhyme, but they're so effective. I finally found out that the "lyrics" are actually a personal's ad someone placed in *The Village Voice* that was set to music. That's why they're so realistic!

Black Boys/White Boys: Three white ladies sing about the joys of black boys and then three black ladies sing about their love of white boys. "Black Boys" is fun because you get to hear Diane Keaton in her only Broadway musical (she sings the solo in the middle of the song), and "White Boys" is phenomenal because of Melba Moore. The song starts out crazily high and then modulates up! Melba Moore was certainly one of the best singers in the show, which is ironic because she almost didn't do it. She was working with the composer Galt MacDermott on a different project, and when he heard her sing, he asked her if she'd be interested in doing HAIR. She glared and said, "I didn't go to four years of music school to do nobody's hair!" FYI: The final lyrics of the song, which are pretty unintelligible, are "mixed media."

TIDBIT TO NAME-DROP TO YOUR FRIENDS: The best version of "Walking in Space" is in the film version. If you've ever seen it, there's a beautiful young Vietnamese girl's voice—but it's actually *not* that girl singing. The beautiful voice you hear is … Betty Buckley's! Betty recorded it, the Vietnamese girl lip-synched, and for some reason, Betty never got credit! Now it can be told! Listen to it and you can totally hear Betty's inflection when she sings "My soul …" She has a Texas twang on "my" (pronounced mah) and her signature tight vowel on "soul" (pronounced "sool").

EXTRA GYPSY TIDBIT Harvey Evans, the king of Broadway Gypsies (seventeen Broadway shows!), played Tulsa during the run of GYPSY and told me that Merman loved corny jokes. And the dirtier, the better. He remembers the touching scene in Act Two where Mama Rose says good-bye to Herbie. Every performance, Merman would cry as she kissed Herbie's forehead. She'd exit into the wings with tears in her eyes, make a beeline to a stagehand and start right up with some version of "There once was a man from Nantucket . . ." Harvey is still impressed by her ability to cry real tears and then immediately start cussing a blue streak.

6. Rent

WHICH VERSION: Though the movie has most of the original Broadway cast, the original cast recording sounds a little more raw (in a good way) and features fabulous Daphne Rubin-Vega as Mimi.

BACKGROUND: Jonathan Larson wrote this updated version of *La Bohème* and set it in the East Village, with Mimi being HIV-positive instead of having consumption. New York Theatre Workshop developed it, but after the final dress rehearsal, Jonathan Larson tragically died of complications from Marfan syndrome. The show though, opened to rave reviews, moved to Broadway, won the Tony Award and the Pulitzer Prize, and became a movie. All over the world, "Rent Heads" are obsessed and see it numerous times.

GAY ASPECT: It's easier to say what isn't gay. The two main leads are straight, as well as a few others, but the whole show is Queer with a capital Q!

BEST SONGS *La Vie Boheme:* Those lyrics! Who hasn't been or known one of those artistic, vegan, we-can-change-the-world types? Listen to the gorgeous section when Roger realizes that Mimi is also HIV-positive.

ROGER: You?
MIMI: Me

Then it sounds like Roger is going to say "Me" again, but after he holds "Me," you realize it's only the first syllable of a word and he's actually saying "Mi-mi." Underneath him the music peacefully resolves. Beautiful.

Seasons of Love: Yes, we've all heard it one thousand times, but that doesn't mean it isn't beautiful. The whole beginning of the song is so creative in its simplicity. Even though it's a group of people, they're not singing some elaborate harmony, they're in pure unison.

TIDBIT TO NAME-DROP TO YOUR FRIENDS: In the middle of "Seasons of Love" there is a soloist who has to hit a high C. Apparently, at one time, there was an understudy who couldn't hit the high C. She was only an emergency understudy and was told she'd never go on. Well, of course, there was an emergency and she had to go on. The cast was all atwitter. What was the understudy going to do when she's supposed to hold that high C for eight counts?

Well, "Seasons of Love" began, and when the section came with the dreaded high C, the understudy decided to opt out of singing completely and filled all eight counts with an improvised rap. That's right, instead of the soloist hitting a long, beautiful high note, she stood, clapped her hands in rhythm. It was probably the only time "Seasons of Love" ended with the whole cast laughing.

---

7. Dreamgirls

WHICH VERSION: You must get all three! The movie has Beyoncé trying to out-sing Jennifer Hudson, and it's a *fierce* battle. The Dreamgirls Concert for The Actor s' Fund (which by now you know I had conducted) is the only full recording of the whole show. The original Broadway cast album features as Effie Tony Award–winner Jennifer Holliday, who owns the part!

BACKGROUND: The team of Henry Kreiger (music) and Tom Eyen (book and lyrics) developed this show, which is obviously based on The Supremes, though it's always been denied. Apparently, nobody wanted to be in court opposite an irate Miss Ross. The show took a while to come together, and the role of Effie went to many different women (it was originally written for Nell Carter!), but once Jennifer Holliday was cast and Michael Bennett took over as director, it all began to coalesce. One of the things that had to be fixed was the fate of Effie. At first, she's kicked out of the girl group because of her weight/bad attitude and wound up dying in Act Two! It was a supreme downer, and the creators realized that audiences want redemption. Effie comes back in Act Two as a calmer, more focused performer and sings "I Am Changing" to illustrate it. By the end, the people who've screwed her over are destroyed, and the girls are all friends again. DREAMGIRLS is groundbreaking for many reasons. First of all, it's a story about black people. Many shows featuring black people are reviews (SMOKEY JOE'S CAFE, AIN'T MISBEHAVIN', BUBBLING BROWN SUGAR), but this is one of the few musicals where all the leads are black and one of the only ones that became successful. Also, the way it was directed was very cinematic. Michael Bennett was able to keep the action flowing continuously, like a film, through the use of rotating light towers that framed the stage. There were no blackouts for set changes, instead the scenes shifted continuously and the show moved at a breakneck speed. It also gave Jennifer Holliday her signature role, winning her a Tony for best actress in a musical.

GAY ASPECT: Essentially the whole creative team (composer, lyricist/book writer, director, choreographer) was gay. Also, what gay man hasn't lip-synched the title song while strutting around the apartment à la *Longtime Companion*?

BEST SONGS: *And I Am Telling You I'm Not Going:* No one has ever topped Jennifer Holliday's performance of this song. Listen and you'll feel compelled to break out into spontaneous applause! To get the full effect of that song, one must listen to the Actors' Fund recording with Lillias White, Audra MacDonald, and Heather Headley, which includes the fight scene that precedes it. The reason the fight is missing from the Broadway cast album is because David Geffen was the producer and wanted it to be more like a pop album. He thought a sung-thru scene was too theatrical. Too theatrical? More like too fabulous! All the main characters bitch it out while hitting crazy-ass high notes. Rumor has it, it almost didn't make the film, but the fates were kind and that belt fest rocks the silver screen.

I Am Changing: This is the song Effie sings at the top of Act Two as she's auditioning for a club in Chicago. Even though she's performing the song, it obviously refers to all she's been through. It's beautifully orchestrated by Harold Wheeler. The song begins with just a rhythm section accompanying Effie, but after she sings "I need a friend . . ." listen to all the violins come in like hope rising from the dead. And by the way, they're real violins, not the horrible synthesizers that have invaded Broadway. The difference to the ear is obvious.

When you listen to it, remember that at first, Effie is auditioning for a club that doesn't want to hear her because of her bad rep. When she's at the big key change and finally sings the word "changing," the lights go from just a close spotlight to completely up, and we see she's no longer auditioning, she's performing in the club surrounded by an audience of fans. It's such a creative way to tell the story without spelling it out.

TIDBIT TO NAME-DROP TO YOUR FRIENDS: Effie's references to "pain" and "not feeling well" and Curtis telling her she's getting fatter all the time is because, unbeknownst to Effie, she's pregnant! We find out in Act Two that she's given birth to Curtis's child! Also, for a short while, "One Night Only" wasn't in the show because Michael Bennett thought it sounded too Jewish. It *is* in a minor key, and the oboe at the beginning does sound a little klezmer. But, so many people were devastated when the song was cut, including the ushers, that it was put back in.

---

8. 1776

WHICH VERSION: Original Broadway cast (as usual!)

BACKGROUND: Sherman Edwards was a history teacher who decided to write a musical about our Founding Fathers. Peter Stone, the book writer of 1776, said that when he would tell people he was working on a show called 1776, it sounded so boring that they would fall asleep between the 17 and the 76! But although it sounds boring it's a GREAT show with a fabulous score. It won the Tony Award for best musical over HAIR, but it's not a stodgy right-wing show. If anything, it's the people who want change, not the conservatives, who are the heroes. The show also gave Gary Beach, one of Broadway's favorite gay men, his first foray on the Great White Way. He took over the role of Rutledge near the end of its run.

GAY ASPECT: 1776 marked the Broadway debut of the twenty-one-year-old Broadway diva Betty Buckley Like in a Hollywood movie, Betty arrived from Texas, found out at the last minute that she had an audition, was the last girl there, and got the gig—all on her *first day in New York*!

BEST SONGS: *But Mr. Adams:* Here's where we find out that it wasn't a noble ideal that made Thomas Jefferson write the Declaration of Independence—

it's because nobody else wanted to do it. I love the campy dialogue in the middle where Jefferson tells Adams he can't write it because he wants to spend the time doing you-know-what with his wife. Adams admits he wants to do the same thing! Not with Mrs. Jefferson, but with Mrs. Adams (I don't think swinging was in vogue during the 1770s). We never think of our forefathers having sex. But this show makes us! And quite frankly, after listening to John Adams's sexy voice, I wouldn't kick him out of *my* ye olde bed. Also, listen to the satisfying harmony at the end of the song on the last word. The top tenor first hits a minor note and then resolves it to major. The tension is punishing and the resolution ... delicious!

He Plays the Violin: Yet another Founding Father sexual reference, this song describes why Martha Jefferson is turned on by Thomas Jefferson. She says that it's not his way with words, but it's his violin playing (insert violin-bow joke here). Sherman Edwards not only wrote a great song, but he imbued it with symbolism. The melody itself is based on the violin. The underlined notes in the phrase "He plays the vi-o-lin" are the intervals of a violin's strings. Neat trick! Betty Buckley had only one scene in the show, and it ended with this song, but it changed the sound of Broadway. Nowadays, in shows like LES MIZ and WICKED, high belting is de rigueur. But in those days, *no one* belted those notes. Betty's bright, piercing belt paved the way for Laurie Beechman, Idina Menzel, and other high beltresses! *Vive la Buckley!*

TIDBIT YOU CAN NAME-DROP TO YOUR FRIENDS: The men in 1776 who do not want independence from Britain are the conservatives. They sing the song "Cool, Cool Considerate Men" with lyrics about staying only on the right and refusing to be on the left. When the film was made, then President Richard Nixon lobbied the producer Jack Warner to cut the song because he thought it could be considered anti-Republican. Nixon's lobbying paid off and the song was cut. Imagine, the media being forced not to make the government look bad. I'm sure that has never re-occurred. Thankfully, the song was restored in the DVD of the film.

9. Company

WHICH VERSION: Original Broadway
BACKGROUND: COMPANY centers around perpetual bachelor Bobby, his friends (who all happen to be couples), and his three girlfriends. The show is not a traditional book show but is made up of various vignettes demonstrating what modern (aka 1970) marriages are like. COMPANY is the first Sondheim musical that Hal Prince directed. They then went on to collaborate on FOLLIES, A LITTLE NIGHT MUSIC, PACIFIC OVERTURES, and SWEENEY TODD. Their work relationship ended acrimoniously with the failure of MERRILY WE ROLL ALONG in the early eighties. They recently teamed up together again for BOUNCE, but that has yet to make it to Broadway. COMPANY was the first show where Sondheim showed his more groovy side, and it gave

Elaine Stritch her signature song, "The Ladies Who Lunch," which is in a great key for any of you young men who need an audition song.

GAY ASPECT: Well, some people think the reason Bobby avoids relationships with his girlfriends is because he's gay, but I say nay to that hogwash because it cheapens the depth of the show. It's very simplistic to say that Bobby doesn't want a woman because he wants a man. The real point of the show is that Bobby is avoiding intimacy because of all the problems he sees in the marriages around him. He struggles with the fact that relationships aren't perfect and that no one person is going to meet all his needs. But what he realizes at the end of the show is that "Being Alive" is about being with another person, whether they ruin your sleep, sit in your chair, etc. The realization is universal. Gay and straight people can identify with wanting a perfect relationship and then maturing enough to realize that nothing is ever perfect. By making him gay, the entire point of the climactic "Being Alive" is moot.

BEST SONGS: *Company:* First of all, it starts with a sound that many of you may not have ever heard—a busy signal. What was modern then makes it sound so time capsule-y now! Then the string of people calling Bobby's name is so creative:

Bobby, Bobby, Bobby baby, Bobby bubbe

Was bubbe ever in a Broadway show before then? It's so New York! This song is also fun to listen to and try to figure out what character is singing what part.

When you get to the part of the song right before the last big chorus, listen especially to when the whole cast sings "We lo-o-o-o-o-o—ove you." I don't know why, but the recording engineers decided to let one voice stick out of that group chord, and it's Elaine Stritch's. She's blatantly flat the whole time . . . but the role she plays in COMPANY is so crotchety and jaded, it actually adds character to what could be a bland chord. But woe to those with perfect pitch! Adjust the volume accordingly.

Another Hundred People: Stephen Sondheim, notorious for writing shows as they rehearse, wrote this song for Pamela Myers after she auditioned. It's perfectly suited to her big-ass range. It also totally captures the pace and excitement yet sometimes loneliness that New York City has in abundance. FYI: . . . "Service" refers to an answering service. I love that 1970s reference . . . There was a time before answering machines and voice mail! Besides the dead-on lyrics and top-notch performance, listen to Jonathan Tunick's orchestrations. Here's the part of the orchestration I love the most: After the song is sung once, it goes back to the bridge. Listen to the trumpets in the background. They're doing quick eighth notes, which are the opening phrase from the song "Company." (Bobby, Bobby, Bobby baby, Bobby bubbe.) He does a subtle musical phrase call-back! No wonder Tunick is always Sondheim's orchestrator.

TIDBIT TO NAME-DROP TO YOUR FRIENDS: The character of Amy, who sings the frenetic "Not Getting Married Today," is Beth Howland, Vera the waitress from TV's Alice. Remember, when she'd be pushed to the brink and steal Flo's comeback? When *she'd* say, "Mel, kiss my grits!" you knew she was *really* pissed off!

Though the lead role of Bobby is sung by Dean Jones, he was going through a divorce at the time and only stayed with the show for a short while. Larry Kert took over early in its run, and even though he was technically a replacement, he was nominated for a Tony Award.

Elaine Stritch sings about the rich ladies who lunch and at one point sings "perhaps a piece of Mahler's." It's an imitation of a lady with too much time on her hands wondering whether she should go see the symphony perform a work by Gustav Mahler. Well, Elaine Stritch may have been brilliant performing this song, but it wasn't until years later that she admitted she had no idea what the reference meant! She thought maybe Mahler's was perhaps a bakery that she had never heard of and the woman was pondering whether to get a piece of cake!

10. Funny Girl

WHICH VERSION: Broadway.

BACKGROUND: FUNNY GIRL is the story of vaudeville comedienne Fanny Brice. The show is about an unconventional-looking girl who becomes a megastar through grit, determination, and incredible talent. Shockingly, even though the parallels are eerie, the role wasn't written for Barbra Streisand. There were *many* other women considered for the role including sixties belter Edie Gorme and Oscar-winner Anne Bancroft! The role finally went to the twenty-one-year-old Barbra, but contrary to what some people think, she wasn't an unknown. She was already a rising star from her brilliant turn as Miss Marmelstein in I CAN GET IT FOR YOU WHOLESALE when she was just nineteen, and her various appearances in clubs and on TV. FUNNY GIRL had mucho trouble out of town, and there were lots of script and songs changes. (One song that was cut, "Absent Minded Me," can be heard on Barbra's *People* CD.) The show lost the best musical Tony Award to HELLO, DOLLY! and similarly, Barbra lost the Tony Award to Carol Channing's portrayal of Dolly Levi.

GAY ASPECT: Three words—Barbra Joan Streisand.

BEST SONGS *Cornet Man:* This is supposed to be a song that Fanny performs in her first solo act in a second-rate show. Of course, Barbra sounds fantastic. She also should get co-composing credit. If you read music, get the score and read along while you listen to Barbra. She completely changes the melody, yet she never gets busted because she always makes it sound better. As a matter of fact, the original rehearsal pianist for FUNNY GIRL was Marvin Hamlisch. He was also in charge of vocal arrangements and at one point complained to Barbra that her changing of the melody in "Sadie, Sadie" was ruining the background harmonies he had written. She looked at him and asked point-blank if the audience was paying money to hear her or his vocal arrangements. Marvin is not a stupid man. He promptly changed the harmonies for the next performance and, not surprisingly, still works with Streisand to this day. Make sure you listen to the section after the big cornet solo (with Barbra in the background awkwardly egging it on . . . "Yeah!" "Whoo!"). Barbra comes back in and sings with such abandon. Today, unfortunately, she seems too concerned with coming off perfect, but back then you can tell she was much freer. To listen to "Cornet Man" is to remind yourself of a much less self-conscious Barbra.

People: This song has been performed at many a wedding and commitment ceremony, not to mention beauty pageant and high-school talent show. There is a problem with a song that becomes a standard: We stop listening to it. We've heard it a thousand times, and it becomes almost like background music. "People" has become one of Barbra's signature songs. She ends almost every concert with it. And, often with an annoying lead-in.

The thing to remember is, the reason a song becomes a standard is because it's good. Listen to "People" and imagine being in the Broadway audience of FUNNY GIRL in 1964. Onstage, there's an oddly beautiful, warm, and talented young woman who has just made her triumphant debut in *The Ziegfeld Follies* and is now on a date with an incredibly handsome, successful man. She turns to him and starts to sing. Listen to the melody and take in the lyrics. Try to imagine how the audience felt hearing that classic being sung to them for the first time. One of the benefits of listening to the Broadway CD and not the movie is how fresh the song still was to Barbra. It wasn't the two millionth time she'd sung it. She had just started doing the show, and there's no affect to her performance. It's pure and honest.

PS: It's also a triumphant song for codependents. We're always being chided for being too needy, and finally there's a song that says, contrary to what our therapists and close friends say, we're actually the luckiest people in the world! Our neediness is our fortune!

TIDBITS TO NAME-DROP TO YOUR FRIENDS: I've said before that Barbra was much less self-conscious then than she is now. But how much less? Listen to the very end of "Don't Rain on My Parade." On the "pa" of "parade," her voice cracks! Let me say it again: Barbra Streisand's voice cracks! Did she do it on purpose to make it sound passionate? Did she not realize it? Did she not have enough power to ask the recording engineers to let her redo it? Who knows? But it's probably the only vocal problem you'll ever hear on a Streisand record.

Now comes something truly bizarre. At the end of "Cornet Man," Barbra sings of a mute that one puts on a cornet called a "wah wah mute." The word "mute" rhymes with the word "suit," in the previous line. For some reason, she decides to change the *t* in the word "mute" to an *l* making it "mule," which not only doesn't rhyme but implies that the cornet player is shoving a mule in his horn. And when you listen to it, note how she overemphasizes it. She doesn't just sing "mule," she sings "mu-u-u-u-LAH!" What was she thinking? Is it her revenge for them refusing to redo her voice crack? Whatever the reason, I can't stop listening to it!

The Off-Broadway CD: Falsettoland

BACKGROUND: FALSETTOLAND is the third musical in the Marvin trilogy (IN TROUSERS and MARCH OF THE FALSETTOS complete the triptych). Marvin is a Jewish man who leaves his wife, Trina, for the athletic and Waspy Whizzer. Falsettoland takes place in 1981 and is about Whizzer contracting an unknown virus, which we know now to be AIDS. "The lesbians from next door," Marvin's good friends, are Dr. Charlotte and her kosher caterer girlfriend, Cordelia. The show is incredibly moving and brilliantly written. This musical gave us the first real, contemporary gay leading men. What's most impressive is that there's no blandly noble man or woman in the show. Each character is flawed just like in real life. Marvin is selfish and Whizzer is a user, but you still know that they truly love each other. One of the main plot points concerns the bar mitzvah of Marvin's son, Jason. Jason wrestles with having a bar mitzvah while Whizzer is so sick. The conflict resolves beautifully when Jason decides to have his Bar Mitzvah in Whizzer's hospital room. As emotionally devastating as this show is, it's also hilarious. Everyone on the CD shows his or her comic chops, with a special shout-out to Faith Prince, who recorded it before she went on to win a Tony Award as Adelaide in GUYS AND DOLLS.

BEST SONGS: *The Baseball Game:* FALSETTOLAND is

"thru-composed," meaning there is no dialogue. Each song is a well-constructed scene and "The Baseball Game" demonstrates that perfectly. We start with Marvin, the "lesbians from next door," Marvin's ex-wife, Trina, and Mendel, her husband, at a baseball game. They're there to watch Marvin's son Jason and other Jewish children "play" baseball. Marvin then sees Whizzer, whom Jason has invited, prompting Trina to ask rhetorically if it's every mother's dream to see the lover of her ex-husband at a Little League game. The song is brilliant because it perfectly expresses both the escalating romantic tension between Whizzer and Marvin during their first meeting since their breakup and Jason's lesson in how to hit the ball. Anyone who has run into an ex can identify, especially when Marvin prays for Whizzer to stand in front of him so he can see Whizzer's bald spot and feel better about himself. Also, listen to Janet Metz's crazy high belt when they all sing about anything being possible at the end of the song. It's a high E!

Unlikely Lovers: This song has both beautiful music and lyrics. Marvin is tending to Whizzer in the hospital and also joking with him about picking up a sailor. Quietly, Charlotte and Cordelia ask if they can come in. The four of them sing a song about how different they all are, yet they're both couples who are also friends. They decide to be scared together, yet also in denial. The contrasts are what make this show so realistic and heartbreaking. And, on top of that, they harmonize like angels! Listen to this song when you want a good cry.

TIDBITS YOU CAN NAME-DROP TO YOUR FRIENDS: After
FALSETTOLAND closed, director Graciela Daniele
directed a version where Act One was MARCH OF
THE FALSETTOS and Act Two was FALSETTOLAND.
It starred Evan Pappas (from MY FAVORITE YEAR)
as Marvin and Roger Bart (from THE PRODUCERS)
as Whizzer. It got great reviews and was slated for
Lincoln Center's Broadway house. Of course, some
people were upset that the people who originated
the roles off-Broadway didn't get their chance
to play them on Broadway, but they weren't in
Daniele's version. Well, some mix-up happened and
the planned Lincoln Center production didn't take
place. Another producing team picked up the idea
of combining both acts, and it opened on Broadway
with the people who created the roles off-Broadway.
Except Barbara Walsh replaced Faith Prince, who
was starring in GUYS AND DOLLS, and Carolee
Carmello replaced Janet Metz, who was starring
in the Canadian version of JOSEPH AND THE
AMAZING TECHNICOLOR DREAMCOAT.

When the show performed on the Tony Awards
(it was nominated for best musical . . . it won for best
score), the producers made the decision to change
some lyrics. The word "lesbians" was changed to the
nonoffensive "people." Phew! Who'd want to hear
the word "lesbians" in a show about gay people?

THE AL HIRSCHFELD THEATRE, NAMED FOR THE FAMOUS
ARTIST, IS ANOTHER OF A NUMBER OF BROADWAY HOUSES
WHOSE NAMES HAVE RECENTLY CHANGED. IT WAS ORIGINALLY
THE MARTIN BECK.

CHAPTER EIGHT

CDs That You Should Own But Have Never Heard Of

If the show's longevity were based only on their singing, it would still be running today!

---

1. The Wild Party (by Andrew Lippa)

WHY?: What a cast! What music!

WHAT THE HELL IS IT?: This show was based on the 1920s poem *The Wild Party* and had the bizarre misfortune to open at the exact same time as *another* musical that was based on the same poem! They wound up being endlessly compared to each other, which doomed them. Both were actually great shows, but the off-Broadway CD is a must-have! The cast consists of steely-voiced Julia Murney making her off-Broadway debut; the fantastic Brian D'Arcy James; Taye Diggs, who had just hit it big in *How Stella Got Her Groove Back* and a pre-WICKED Idina Menzel.

DON'T MISS: Those four beeyatches singing their lungs out in "The Juggernaut," Idina tearing up "The Life of the Party," and Julia raising the roof in "Raise the Roof." There's also the always hilarious Alix Korey, who plays a 1920s butch lesbian and sings the knee-slapping "An Old-fashioned Love Story. "

---

2. Zanna Don't

WHY?: So gay! So fantastic!

WHAT THE HELL IS IT?: Don't be fooled by the cutesy title. This is one of the most moving yet joyful off-Broadway musicals. The show is about a high school that is in the opposite universe from ours. Everybody is gay. When a guy and gal decide to come out as straight, everyone turns against them, except resident cupid Zanna. À la *A Tale of Two Cities,* Zanna decides to sacrifice his magic powers to make the world safe for straight people. Because of his sacrifice, though, Zanna finally finds love in the last scene. It may sound sappy, but while I listen on the treadmill, I have to wipe tears from my eyes! The fantastic cast is led by pre–*Queer Eye* Jai Rodriguez as Zanna, and everyone else has a chance to shine, especially the brassy belter, Anika Larson.

DON'T MISS: *Ain't Got Time:* Anika Larson sings this song of lesbian defiance. Listen to how long she holds the last note. Don't try it at home without an oxygen tank.

Whatcha Got?: Since the high school is basically in Bizarro World, the cool kids are the chess champions, and this whole ultra-sexy and exciting song is a big cheer to get the local chess nerd (who's considered big man on campus) to win. The song builds and builds, and you will find yourself funking out with it and suddenly thinking Bobby Fisher is a hottie.

3. Snoopy! (London Cast!)

WHY?: Songs you will love!

WHAT THE HELL IS IT?: Snoopy is like a sequel to the off-Broadway hit, YOU'RE A GOOD MAN, CHARLIE BROWN, except it's by a totally different creative team. The music is by Larry Grossman and the lyrics are by Hal Hackady. The songs are super tuneful, and the performances are full of charm. One of the fun parts, besides the songs, is listening to the words where the British people don't quite master the American accent. Listen to the song "Clouds." Lucy says you can see "all sorts of things" in the clouds, but she says the word "sorts" less like an American girl and more like a hoity-toity Dame Judy Dench.

DON'T MISS: *Edgar Allan Poe:* All the kids are in class, and the girls are panicked because they know nothing about the assignment and they're dreading being called on by Miss Othmar. Peppermint Patty (Nicky Croyden) in the first character singing, and she has the kind of voice I love! A little nasal with a fast vibrato. I can't get enough! Linus knows all the answers, and Charlie Brown keeps chiming in with completely wrong information. I'm obsessed with the fervency of Peppermint Patty trying to save her ass at the end of the song by offering to spell Mississippi, which she does by spelling it "M-I-S-S-S-S-S-S-S-S-I-P-P-I!"

I Know Now: Peppermint Patty, Sally, and Lucy sing about what they know now that they're older (and by older, they mean still in the single digits). The melody is so infectious and the lyrics, hilarious! Lucy has learned that a smile makes a bad umbrella and, after they all sing off-pitch with no accompaniment, they realize they've learned not to sing a cappella. They get mad props for that! Shout-out to music majors everywhere! Using the phrase "a cappella" as a lyric!?!?! I've never heard that in a song before or since!

4. Chess

WHY?: A one-of-a-kind score with one-of-a-kind singers.

WHAT THE HELL IS IT?: Everyone knows about the Broadway hit MAMMA MIA. But the men of ABBA who wrote that score haven't always been raking in the Broadway bucks. They had a big, fat flop in the 1980s. CHESS opened and closed in the spring of 1988. The plot centered on the Cold War, using a chess tournament to demonstrate the tension between the East and the West. When the show first ran in London in the early eighties the Cold War was in full swing, but it started fading out in the late eighties, and the script was altered and wound up not making sense/being too boring. When the show went on tour in 1989, the Cold War was so changeable, they actually brought along a writer to keep the show current! Even though the musical didn't last, the CD remains. It starred three of the best singers from Broadway: Judy Kuhn, Phillip Casnoff, and the late David Carroll. Judy was the original Cossette in LES MIZ, where she sang the high soprano notes of an ingénue. In CHESS, she is a Broadway belter of the highest degree! Phillip Casnoff sings phenomenally but is best known as the actor who got clobbered by the set of SHOGUN: THE MUSICAL during a performance that was being reviewed! (He recovered, but the show didn't.) David Carroll had done some Broadway shows before CHESS but didn't hit it big till he starred as the Baron in GRAND HOTEL a few years later. If the show's longevity were only based on their singing, it would still be running today!

DON'T MISS: *Someone Else's Story:* CHESS had been done in London and starred Elaine Paige, but when it came to Broadway, a song was added for Judy Kuhn. The melody is gorgeous and Judy's performance is stunning. I loved this song till it became a big audition piece for girls in the early nineties and I had to play it a thousand times a day. Then I grew to hate it. But, thankfully, I haven't played it for a gaggle of girls in a while, so I'm back to loving it.

Anthem: David Carroll closed Act One with this.

He played a Russian chess player who decides to defect. This song tells of the love he'll always have for his country and, once again, the melody is gorgeous. Add to that David Carroll's thrilling tone, and you will listen to this over and over!

---

5. The Mystery of Edwin Drood

WHY?: Singers at the top of their game.

WHAT THE HELL IS IT?: THE MYSTERY OF EDWIN DROOD is based on a Charles Dickens book that was never finished. So, every night the musical had a different ending. The audience would vote on who they thought the murderer was, and whoever was deemed the dastardly killer would sing a song describing why they did it. The show started at the Public Theater and was performed in Central Park before transferring to Broadway, and it was nominated for numerous Tony Awards. The book, music, lyrics, *and* orchestrations were written by Rupert Holmes. He is best known for writing "Escape (The Pina Colada Song)" and the TV series *Remember WENN.* At one point he was also going to star in the show but was talked out of it! Nobody can pull that off except Streisand. The show CD is a gem because of the performances of Betty Buckley and Howard McGillan. The concept of the show is that a troupe of English music hall actors are putting on THE MYSTERY OF EDWIN DROOD, and as was the fashion of the day, the leading lady plays the leading man. Betty Buckley played the role of Drood, and Howard McGillan played Neville, her friend/

nemesis. Patti Cohenour is lovely as the ingénue, and jazz singer Cleo Lane plays the opium addict Princess Puffer. FYI: She was replaced by Loretta "Hot Lips Hoolihan" Switt.

DON'T MISS: *Two Kinsmen:* Howard and Betty sing of their lifelong friendship and essentially spend the song out-belting each other. Listen carefully to their vowels. So many singers have to modify an "oo" sound. Instead of singing "true" they'll sing "trow," or they'll sing "yow" instead of "you" to open the vowel and make it easier to sing. But Howard and Betty stay true to the vowel and make the song that much more exciting!

Perfect Strangers: Betty Buckley and Patti Cohenour profess their love for each other. Although this sounds like a lesbian love duet, it's not. Remember, Betty is playing a man! Patti sings with her sweet, natural soprano, and Betty modifies her massive belt to make their voices blend superbly. My favorite part is the end where they sing "ahh" and the chords change underneath them. Beautiful!

The Writing on the Wall: This is one of the greatest performances of Betty's career. The character of Edwin Drood reveals that he hasn't been murdered, just assaulted. He feigns death in order to find out who tried to kill him. The song implores the audience to appreciate their lives and live in the now. Betty begins the song by speaking in rhythm and slowly introduces her singing voice. By the end, she is singing triumphantly and brings it all to a climax when she hits the high note . . . a full-voiced, perfectly placed, high E . . . Á CAPPELLA!!!!!

Betty said the song was supposed to end on a lower note, and one day at rehearsal she popped out the note just for fun and the cast freaked out. "How did you do that??? You *have* to put that in the show!" And she did! And my life was complete!

6. Merrily We Roll Along

WHY?: One of Sondheim's best scores.

WHAT THE HELL IS IT?: Sondheim wrote the score, George Furth wrote the book (based on a play by Kauffman and Hart), Hal Prince directed the show, and critics destroyed it. It told the story of a composer, lyricist, and novelist whose friendship disintegrates as they become successful. The story is told backwards from the 1980s to the 1950s. The problems with the show lie with the book, and though the show has been revived and revised throughout the years, a successful version still hasn't emerged. However, the score is brilliant! From the opening trumpets of the overture to the beautiful harmonies of "Our Time," this is Sondheim at his best. The show only ran for sixteen performances and the album was recorded the day after the show closed, so the performers had to have been quite emotional in the recording studio. The vulnerability pays off, and everyone gives a stunning performance. The show also launched the careers of Liz Callaway, Lonny Price, Jim Walton, Ann Morrison, and *Seinfeld*'s Jason Alexander. It also broke up the professional relationship of Hal Prince and Stephen Sondheim, who didn't work together again until after the millennium!

DON'T MISS: *Good Thing Going:* This is a beautiful love song about a relationship that goes wrong. Lonny Price has one of my favorite brassy, Broadway, slightly cantor-esque voices. The composing team in the show perform this at a party and are begged to do an encore after the first performance. Listen to the brilliant way Sondheim shows the party-goers losing interest in the song as it's repeated.

Opening Doors: This is my favorite song in the show. It showcases Sondheim's brilliant lyric writing and tells a continuous story throughout the song. Charlie, Frank, and Mary have all just moved to New York and are writing, creating, meeting bad boyfriends, getting exciting jobs, getting loser jobs, and going through what everyone has gone thorough when he/she is first starting out. I'd always been obsessed with the voice of the producer who tells the composing team that their music isn't hummable enough. My favorite singer grew up to be George Castanza! Jason Alexander was in his early twenties when he landed this gig. He then went on to THE RINK (another unsuccessful show) and finally got the lead in JEROME ROBBINS' BROADWAY for which he won the Tony Award for best actor in a musical, which in turn led him to *Seinfeld*. In 2001, he hosted a reunion concert of the original cast. It was very poignant because when the show opened in 1981, all the actors were in their early twenties playing characters who begin the show in their forties and age backwards. At the reunion concert, they began the show at their real ages and aged backwards to the age when they first performed the show.

7. The Most Happy Fella

WHY?: Beautiful story/beautiful score.

WHAT THE HELL IS IT?: THE MOST HAPPY FELLA has music and lyrics by Frank Loesser, who also wrote GUYS AND DOLLS and HOW TO SUCCEED IN BUSINESS WITHOUT REALLY TRYING. It's based on the play THEY KNEW WHAT THEY WANTED and the story, including a pregnancy from a one-night stand, seems very advanced for the 1950s. Remember, this is the decade that wouldn't allow Lucy to say the word "pregnant" on TV. She had to say "expecting."

When THE MOST HAPPY FELLA was casting, many young sopranos auditioned for the lead ingénue role (including Florence Henderson!), but it went to Jo Sullivan, who then went on to marry the composer, the much older Frank Loesser. The show ran for years and has been revived on Broadway twice and recently at New York City Opera with Paul Sorvino. The show preceded the 1980's trend of the sung-thru musical. Even though there is dialogue, it's all underscored by the orchestra. Since the dialogue and music are so intertwined, the whole show was recorded, start to finish! It's available on a two-CD set, and you should try to listen to it from the beginning so you follow the story, which will leave you weepy at the end!

DON'T MISS: *Ooh, My Feet:* The show begins with a waitress complaining about being on her feet all night. Susan Johnson, who plays Cleo, had one of my favorite Broadway voices. I not only love the sound of it, but after you listen to just one of her songs, you'll want to be friends with her! This is actually the first song I ever became obsessed with. I recently found a tape of myself singing it when I was a few days shy of three years old!

The Most Happy Fella: The leading role of Tony was played by operatic baritone Robert Weede. Normally, I don't like opera singers' voices because of the "covered" sound they go for, but I *love* Weede's voice! So natural and clear! So bright! Listen to the last note. Not only is it a high G, which is slightly above a baritone's range, but it's on an *e* vowel! *E* vowels are notoriously difficult to sing because they tighten you up. That's why so many bad singers change the word "me" to "may." Also, Frank Loesser gave a tip o' the hat to some of the cast in the lyrics. Listen to the postman calling out names of people in the town. He calls for Johnson (as in Susan) and for Sullivan (as in Jo)!

8. Side Show

WHY?: Two Tony–nominated performances.

WHAT THE HELL IS IT?: SIDE SHOW has a script and lyrics by Bill Russell, who was one of the writers of the hilarious off-Broadway show PAGEANT. The music is by Henry Kreiger who composed DREAMGIRLS. The show is based on the story of Daisy and Violet Hilton (played by Emily Skinner and Alice Ripley), who were conjoined twins and became singing-and-dancing stars during the Depression. The show only ran one hundred performances but was nominated for a Tony Award for best musical, best score, and Alice Ripley and Emily Skinner shared a nomination as best actress. Emily and Alice performed the show side by side, singing gorgeous harmony and doing intricate dance moves. Although it looked like they were taped together or had special costumes built, they simply stood hip to hip and stayed connected the whole time.

DON'T MISS: *Who Will Love Me As I Am?*: By the end of Act One, the girls are maturing and wondering if anyone will ever love them. They know they're different and fear that people won't see past their "freakishness" to love them for who they are. This song speaks to every gay person who grew up fearing they would always be alone. It also speaks to every gay person who loves fierce singing! Work it, girls!

I Will Never Leave You: By the end of Act Two, the twins have been betrayed and stand alone onstage. They comfort each other with the knowledge that no matter how hard life gets, they will always be there for each other. I love David Chase's vocal arrangement, because instead of singing in pure harmony (three notes away from each other), they sing in fourths. They performed this song on the 1998 Tony Awards. See if you can get a copy because they make a huge mistake at the beginning. By the time the Tony Awards came, the show had been closed for months, and it was very emotional putting on the costumes again and singing this song. Instead of singing the proper first lyric, Alice Ripley sang a lyric that happens much later in the song but spoke of her state of mind, "I'm scared!" Emily covered, and Alice got right back on track and the song soared. But if you watch the beginning you can see the panic on their faces and it's what makes live theater exciting!

9. The Last Five Years

WHY?: Great score, great performances.

WHAT THE HELL IS IT?: Jason Robert Brown won a Tony Award for writing the score to PARADE, but I love his off-Broadway score even more. Jason was a quickly rising composer who married a struggling actress and got divorced after five years. He then wrote a musical about a quickly rising author who marries a struggling actress and gets divorced after five years. Similar? You decide. Regardless, the music and lyrics are fabulous, as are the two leads. Sherie Rene Scott is that rare creature who can do comedy, drama, sing up a storm, and is beautiful. Her husband was played by the pre-Tony Award–winning Norbert Leo Butz. He's charming and funny, with a unique sound that I love. There is no dialogue in the show, only song. It was directed by Hal Prince's daughter, Daisy. And like Mr. Prince's show MERRILY WE ROLL ALONG, it's told backwards. Well, Sherie tells her story backwards, while Norbert tells his forwards. So, at the beginning of the show, Sherie is dealing with the recent breakup of the marriage and Norbert is about to meet the girl he will marry. Jason is the pianist on the CD and his orchestrations are *incredible*! Listen to what he can do with his string players!

DON'T MISS: *Movin' Too Fast:* This is Norbert's first song, and it describes his accelerated ascension into writing fame. It's jazzy and driving, and Norbert has some sassy riffs in the middle. I'm totally obsessed with his hard *r*'s. Listen to how he pronounces "skater" and "later." You'll hear "skateRRR" and "lateRRR" I love it! FYI: It's very similar to Emily Skinner's hard *r*'s in SIDESHOW, which I also love. Listen to her "Like Everyone Else" and you'll hear her sing "sisteRRR," and in "Leave Me Alone" you'll hear "motheRRR". Grip those *r*'s, baby!

Summer in Ohio: This song is a letter that Sherie is writing to Norbert while she is doing summer stock in Ohio. Jason has a great lyric that describes summer stock perfectly. Usually you have a small troupe of actors who play a multitude of roles throughout the summer, some appropriate, some inappropriate. Sheri sings of a fellow actor who's playing both Tevye (an old Jew) and Porgy (a young black man)! Hilarious! Also, listen to her last few notes . . . a fabulous belted E-flat and blues riff at the end.

10. A New Brain

WHY?: Beautiful score, moving story.

WHAT THE HELL IS IT?: After William Finn wrote the FALSETTO's trilogy, he didn't write much else. Suddenly, he had something wrong with his brain and almost died. He regretted all the time he had wasted not writing and started composing up a storm. His first foray was turning his near death into a musical. When it was done as a reading at The

Public Theater, it was a song cycle. Because it didn't have a fully developed plot, James Lapine (INTO THE WOODS) was called in to fill in the holes. It told the story of Gordon Schwinn (aka William Finn) who is a composer who's wasting his life writing for a children's TV show. After a brain ailment nearly kills him, he realizes he should be writing all kinds of music and stop being so crabby all the time! The show didn't have a successful run, but the CD is great! Malcolm Gets plays Gordon (originally Michael Rupert in the first reading), and Penny Fuller, who played Eve Harrington in APPLAUSE, plays Gordon's mother (performed by Dorothy Loudon and Nancy Dussault in earlier readings). Great singers fill out the rest of the cast including a pre-Glinda Kristin Chenoweth as the bitchy nurse!

DON'T MISS: *Heart and Music:* This song essentially takes place in Gordon's head as he undergoes treatment in the ICU. Not only are the melody and lyrics great, but so is the vocal arrangement. Why? Because the vocal arranger was Tony Award–winning composer, Jason Robert Brown, and he went to town with the harmonies. Listen to the cool a cappella section near the end of the song! It takes me back to the a cappella section in *Fame*'s "I Sing The Body Electric."

Sailing: One of the best male singers on Broadway is Norm Lewis. His velvet voice is part legit/part gospel. He stepped in at the last minute because the original actor who opened the show had a vocal injury. Norm learned the score super quick, recorded the CD, and took over the role. This song is based on William Finn's real-life boyfriend, who goes sailing to relax. If you want to know how much Finn enjoys sailing, listen to the song called "Sitting Becalmed." Hint: He hates it!

#4

Know Your Divas

1 Betty Buckley likes to be called:

   a. Betty Sue
   b. Betty Lynn
   c. Betty Bob
   d. Ms. Grizabella

2. Bernadette Peters sister is a famous:

   a. Acrobat in Cirque du Soleil
   b. Reality TV star
   c. Casting director
   d. Sister? This diva's an only child!

Know Your Divas

3. Patti LuPone's brother starred in which long-running musical?

    a. EVITA: *He was Juan Peron, Eva's husband*

    b. A CHORUS LINE: *He was Zach, the director*

    c. SUNDAY IN THE PARK WITH GEORGE: *He played George after Mandy Patinkin*

    d. CATS: *He was Unoteste...the half-neutured male*

4. How old was Jennifer Holliday when she won the Tony Award for playing Effie?

    a. 21
    b. 29
    c. 30
    d. 40

5. Name the female star who has all these musicals in common: BYE BYE BIRDIE, West Side Story, Bajour, and Kiss of the Spider Woman.

SHUBERT THEATRE
MONTY PYTHON'S SPAMALOT
BEST MUSICAL

MILFORD PLAZA

BROADHURST

MONTY PYTHON'S

BEST MUSICAL   2005 Tony Award

THE FLAGSHIP THEATRE FOR THE SHUBERT ORGANIZATION, THE SAM S. SHUBERT THEATRE HAS A STORIED HISTORY. *A CHORUS LINE* PLAYED HERE; NOW IT'S HOME TO *MONTY PYTHON'S SPAMALOT.*

CHAPTER NINE

Keep It Gay! The Gay Characters of Broadway

As a matter of fact, rather than letting the understudy or standby go on for Hugh when he was on vacation, the producers instead opted to close the show for two weeks!

NAME: All the boys in the band except Alan (wink, wink)

SHOW: THE BOYS IN THE BAND

SEXUAL ORIENTATION: Shhh .... THE BOYS IN THE BAND was THE groundbreaking play for gay people. It opened off-Broadway in 1968 and ran for one thousand performances. The play takes place during a birthday party that Michael is throwing for Harold. One of his presents is a male hustler named "Cowboy" because Harold may have trouble finding sexual partners now that he's turning thirty. Is thirty still considered old? If so, uh-oh. The dialogue moves from bitchy to mean as the guests get drunker, and the play ends with each having to play a game that requires him to telephone someone and declare his love for them. Though some folks dismiss this show as a negative portrayal of homosexuality, I feel that it has to be seen in context. This play was written *before* Stonewall. Gayness was not spoken about except in the hushed whispers of THE CHILDREN'S HOUR. The playwright, Mart Crowley, gave a voice to many different types of gay men, including one couple and one man who maintains he's straight but we're meant to think the lady doth protest too much.

A film was made in 1970 and author/producer Crowley insisted that the off-Broadway cast be used. It was directed by William Friedkin, who then went on to make *The French Connection, The Exorcist,* and, unfortunately, *Cruising*. Rent it to see what gay life looked like in the late sixties and hear the nonstop bons mots and bitchy-ass put downs. Make sure you watch it with a group of your friends so you can assign each one a character they most resemble. This will undoubtedly lead to a big, fat fight or a twenty-minute crying jag.

NAME: Duane
SHOW: APPLAUSE
SEXUAL ORIENTATION: Gay
APPLAUSE is the musical version of the Oscar-winning film, *All About Eve*. Margo Channing, the role that

Bette Davis created in the film, was played by Lauren Bacall in her first musical. Margo is a Broadway star who befriends and is ultimately betrayed by a young actress named Eve Harrington, played in the musical by Penny Fuller. Margo's fun-loving assistant Duane was played by triple-threat Lee Roy Reams. Early in the show Eve Harrington appears at Margo's stage door, and Margo decides to take her out for a night on the town. She invites Duane to come with them, but he demurs because he has a "date." Lauren Bacall then uttered what was probably scandalously titillating to an audience in 1970 ... "Bring him along!" Thus follows "But Alive" ... the only number ever in a Broadway show to take place in a gay bar! Kudos to the creative team for putting a gay character in a musical!

NAME: Paul San Marcos
SHOW: A CHORUS LINE
SEXUAL ORIENTATION: Gay

As discussed in Chapter Seven, A CHORUS LINE was created by long rap sessions with a big group of Broadway dancers. These sessions began at midnight and ended in the morning. One of the dancers, Nicholas Dante, told his story, which was pretty much transcribed verbatim and became the monologue for Paul. He speaks of being a young gay man who learns that one can be effeminate and still be a man. When he parents unexpectedly show up backstage at one of his shows and see him dressed in drag, he is devastated. But he then hears his father ask the producer to "take care of his son." Paul breaks down as he reveals it was the first time his father called him that. For many young gay people, Paul was the first major character they ever encountered who was openly gay. This was before Will, Jack, *Making Love*, and the *Brokeback* cowboys. All they had was Uncle Arthur and his beard, Sarina. People have faulted the show because Paul winds up being the character who injures himself and possibly will never dance again. Most self-respecting homosexuals reject the cliché of the doomed gay man. However, I think the reason that Paul was chosen to be the one who falls is because he is the character we feel the most for. If an injury happened to one of the other male characters, it wouldn't have the same impact. The audience grows to care about Paul during his monologue, so the creators chose him to be the one who gets hurt in order to have the maximum dramatic impact. The good news is, during the "One" finale, Paul is the first one who comes out dancing, and in the famous triangle position (it's the photo used on one of the posters), he's always in the front point, so I guess his injuries heal in the last fifteen minutes of the show!

NAME: EVERYONE
SHOW: LOVE! VALOR! COMPASSION!
SEXUAL ORIENTATION: Gay, gay, GAY!!!
LVC, as it's called on savvy theater message boards, is by out playwright, Terrence McNally who gave us THE LISBON TRAVIATA, MASTER CLASS, THE RITZ, and the books to many musicals including

RAGTIME and KISS OF THE SPIDER WOMAN. LVC has also been called the 1990's BOYS IN THE BAND because it centers around a group of gay men in a "relaxing" setting. The three acts take place in a country house shared by an aging choreographer and his blind boyfriend who invite their gay friends out for three holiday weekends, Memorial Day, the Fourth of July, and Labor Day. There is much love, betrayal, and naked penises throughout, as well as a Hispanic dancer/possible hustler, a monogamous couple, and a show tune–loving costume designer originally played by Nathan Lane (replaced by Mario Cantone in his first Broadway role). Though there is a similarity to BOYS IN THE BAND, there is only one self-loathing character, as opposed to the entire cast of the earlier play. Also, because it's the nineties, HIV is an underlying theme. It won the Tony Award for best play of 1995, and many people were shocked when it didn't win the Pulitzer Prize. The movie, unfortunately, went on to receive only tepid reviews, but it's worth renting it if you've never seen the play. The whole original cast reprised their roles, but Nathan Lane, had a conflict and wound up being unable to do the film, causing a big rift in the friendship between him and McNally. Jason Alexander took over the role in the film, thereby giving it some name recognition and also appeared in a tutu, thereby giving it some horrifying imagery. FYI: McNally and Lane have mended their fences, and McNally is still writing plays for him.

NAME: Roger DeBris and Carmen Ghia
SHOW: THE PRODUCERS
SEXUAL ORIENTATION: Gay

THE PRODUCERS is about two guys who decide to produce the worst musical imaginable so it will close and they can keep all the investors' money. They decide to produce *Springtime for Hitler* and hire Roger DeBris, the worst director ever. They go to the Upper East Side, where they're greeted by Mr. DeBris's "common-law" assistant, Carmen Ghia. Roger Bart originated the role of Carmen, and at the audition he was given the scene where he opens the door and says "Yesss?" He decided to elongate the *s* way past what was in the script to gay-ify the character, and that's what got him the job. If you got a chance to see him do it on Broadway, you would have seen him extend it for at least fifteen seconds and pause. As soon as Nathan Lane would finally try to speak, Roger would come back in aggresively with another dose of "S-s-s-s-s." It always brought the house down. Gary Beach won a Tony Award for his portrayal of Roger DeBris and, like Roger Bart, re-created it for the film. His character is anything but one note. I love how unfeminine he is in the first scene, even though he's dressed for the choreographer's ball in a full gown. Most actors would choose to play him ultra-girly, but Gary Beach clunked around the stage like a linebacker in Vera Wang. He also channels various divas when he's forced to go on as Adolph in "Spingtime for Hitler." Listen to the CD when he pronounces the words "greater" and "dictator." He makes an especially hard *r*, which he told me was his tip o' the hat to Mary Martin. All in all, these two took roles that could have been unbearably offensive and instead made the comedy about their characters, not their gayness.

NAME: Zsa Zsa/Albin
SHOW: LA CAGE AUX FOLLES
ORIENTATION: Gay (with one straight dalliance)

LA CAGE AUX FOLLES was a French movie that was adapted into a musical by a gay trio. Harvey Fierstein wrote the book, Jerry Herman wrote the music and lyrics, and Arthur Laurents directed it. It tells the story of Georges, who runs a club in the south of France with his partner, Albin, who is the lead drag performer Zsa Zsa. Georges has a son from his one-night detour with a woman, whom he and Albin raise together. When their son gets engaged to a girl from a "conservative" (read: homophobic) family, he asks that Albin not be at the engagement dinner. The show is a major milestone for positive gay visibility for many reasons. First of all, the relationship between the two men is multilayered and presented to the audience as deep and loving. Georges sings of when he first met and fell in love with Albin in the beautiful "Song on the Sand." This was the first ever love song on Broadway between two men, paving the way for FALSETTOS and RENT. Also, Georges reprimands his son in "Look Over There" for not acknowledging the wonderful parenting he got from Albin. This show debuted in 1983 and gay adoption is *still* not legal in many states, so you can see how LA CAGE was way ahead of its time. The big, gay anthem happens at the end of Act One when Albin finds out that the mother of Georges's son, who had nothing to do with his upbringing, will be at the engagement dinner yet Albin is not invited. He turns his self-pity, sadness, and rage into the gay pride–filled "I Am What I Am," effectively saying, "So what if I'm different? I'm still a valuable person, and everyone else needs to adjust his or her view of the world" . . . but not as awkwardly stated. Gary Beach played the role in the revival and was nominated for a Tony, and George Hearn originated it, winning the Tony Award for best actor in a musical.

NAME: Arnold Beckoff
SHOW: TORCH SONG TRILOGY
SEXUAL ORIENTATION: Gay

Harvey Fierstein was a downtown performer who made his acting debut in 1971, when he was a teenager, in Andy Warhol's only play. Fierstein wrote three one-act plays between 1976 and 1979 that became the three acts of TORCH SONG TRILOGY. The shows began downtown at La MaMa, moved off-Broadway, and then took Broadway by storm in the early eighties. He is the first person to have won a Tony Award for best actor and best play for the same show. The show is about Arnold, a professional drag queen, as he searches for romantic love in New

York City, as well as acceptance from his mother. Since the show was written mainly in the 1970s, the most horrifying thing Arnold has to deal with is gay bashing, which seemed so innocent once AIDS reared its ugly head. Arnold is like a combination of That Girl and Lucy Ricardo. Until that point, gay characters were either off to the side of the main characters or off-Broadway. Arnold was the first gay, leading-man role on Broadway. Why did audiences accept him? Fierstein says, "Everyone wants what Arnold wants: an apartment they can afford, a job they don't hate too much, a chance to go to the store once in a while, and someone to share it all with." People were able to see a gay person as a person like them. As the original producer of TORCH SONG put it, " . . . what Harvey proved was that you could use a gay context and a gay experience and speak in universal truths."

TORCH SONG TRILOGY was turned into a movie, with Fierstein writing the screenplay and re-creating his role. His Jewish mother was played by Anne Bancroft . . . not Jewish, but she was married for years to Mel Brooks. The male model Arnold has a relationship with was played by Matthew Broderick, who had originally played the troubled teen in the show when it was off-Broadway. TORCH SONG certainly gave the plight of gay men more focus than it ever had on Broadway up to that point. But perhaps TORCH SONG's greatest contribution to the gay man's coterie was the discovery of the actress who played Arnold's mother. She had no experience. She was a housewife. This woman, plucked from obscurity, soon went on to create the role of Sofia on *The Golden Girls*! Yes, I'm talking about the acting debut of Estelle Getty! It all began in TORCH SONG TRILOGY! Brava, Harvey!

NAMES: Joanne, Maureen, Angel, Collins
SHOW: RENT
SEXUAL ORIENTATION: Lesbian, bisexual, gay

Jonathan Larson wanted to change the face of Broadway and he did. He adapted the opera *La Bohème* into a rock musical that took place in the Lower East Side during the early nineties, which was the age of AIDS before protease inhibitors. FALSETTOS portrayed the New York yuppie gay, RENT showed us the young, hot, sexy, hemp-smoking (and wearing) queer. The groundbreaking aspect of this show is how it has been embraced by teenagers the world over. The show is seen again and again by these self-named "Rent Heads." They root for the relationship between the drag queen Angel and his lover Collins as much as they do for Roger and Mimi. They cheer when they hear Broadway's first lesbian love duet ("Take Me or Leave Me"), and they cry when Angel finally passes away. RENT empowers the young gay person wondering if he or she will ever fit it. It gives him/her confidence to be whatever he/she is by witnessing gay people portrayed onstage and embraced by fellow teenagers. What's wonderful is the broad array of gay that's on the stage. These characters aren't just gay, they're uptight (Joanne), flaky/flirty/cheaty/bi (Maureen) peacemakers (Angel), and anarchists

(Collins). And who says playing gay is bad for your career? The show led to Jesse L. Martin (Collins) starring in *Law and Order* and to Wilson Jermaine Heredia receiving a Tony Award for his performance as Angel. Also, Idina Menzel (Maureen) went on to win a Tony for WICKED, and *Queer Eye for the Straight Guy*'s Jai Rodriguez first got on the radar by being a replacement for Angel on Broadway. People with HIV who live and love, lesbians who have fights while belting Es, and drag queens who rap while wearing crazy high-heeled boots . . . long live RENT!

CHARACTER: Peter Allen
SHOW: THE BOY FROM OZ
SEXUAL ORIENTATION: Bi

Peter Allen was a composer and performer who hailed from Austalia or "Oz." He not only headlined in sold-out concerts all over the world where he would sing and accompany himself on the piano, he also wrote lots of hit pop songs like "Arthur's Theme" (sung by Christopher Cross) and "Don't Cry Out Loud" (sung by Melissa Manchester). THE BOY FROM OZ could be classified as a jukebox musical, since it used preexisting music from an artist (Peter Allen) and then placed those songs in a story (the life of Peter Allen). While the show got middling reviews, it made Hugh Jackman a huge Broadway star. Previously, Hugh had starred in the Australian version of THE BOY FROM OZ, then went on to play Curly in the London production of OKLAHOMA! But those of us stateside only knew him from his portrayal of Wolverine, the steely-eyed, metal-clawed mutant in the *X-Men* film franchise. The character of Peter Allen was vastly different from what most people had seen him do in the movies, as Wolverine never played keyboards, shook his mutant ass, or did Rockette-style kicks. But Hugh Jackman did *all* of that. He became the darling of Broadway and even hosted the Tony Awards twice. But who was Peter Allen? Besides being a world-famous entertainer, Peter was a gay-leaning bisexual, who had the distinction to hang out with Judy Garland *and* marry Liza Minnelli when she was twenty. His relationship with Liza takes up the early part of Act One (the real Liza never saw the show), but THE BOY FROM OZ didn't shy away from the fact that Peter had relationships with men. His dying lover sings him a love song in Act Two, and Peter's death from AIDS ends the show. Although, right after Peter dies, he descends from Heaven on a piano-note staircase, dressed all in white, singing "I Go To Rio," and the love song that his lover sings is "I Honestly Love You." So, if one wasn't satisfied with just the acknowledgement of Peter's gayness, there was also a severely campy quality that pervaded everything (unfortunately possibly without the creators intending it.) But, regardless of the show itself, critics and audiences agreed, Hugh Jackman's performance was world class. I saw it well into its run, and it was as if it were opening night. His onstage freshness and energy was something I'd rarely seen past the first month of a show. Broadway grande dame Barbara Cook was so obsessed with Jackman's performance that she saw the show thirteen times! As a matter of fact, rather than letting the understudy or standby go on for Hugh when he was on vacation, the producers instead opted to close the show for two weeks! That's never been done on Broadway before, but Hugh Jackman was a force of nature that the producers felt couldn't be equaled.

NAME: Celie
SHOW: THE COLOR PURPLE
SEXUAL ORIENTATION: Lesbian

THE COLOR PURPLE began as a book by Alice Walker that told of the long-suffering life of Celie, a southern woman in the early 1900s. In the book, Celie finally starts to find her happiness when she begins a relationship with Shug, a sassy jazz singer. The Steven Spielberg movie starred Whoopi Goldberg and, not surprisingly, took out the lesbian subplot. It was way too shocking to have a lesbian love story in a movie. After all, the film came out in the 1940s. Oh wait, it came out in the 1980s. Turns out, there's no excuse . . . . Anyhoo, the musical came to Broadway in 2005 and put the lesbianism back in the story. We see the desire on Celie's face when she gives the nude Shug a bath. They end Act One with a love song and a smooch. They don't quite wind up together at the end because Shug craves male attention, but their relationship is shown as something beautiful. Miss Oprah herself invested one million dollars into the show, which changed its name to "Oprah Winfrey presents THE COLOR PURPLE." Because of Oprah's involvement, and because the whole cast is black, the show attracts a large black audience. Broadway has always been a place where white people go. When I sit in a pit orchestra and look in the house, I see a sea of white faces. THE COLOR PURPLE not only is able to get black people to the theater, but makes them cheer and support a lesbian relationship! The show was led by the brilliant Tony Award–winning actress, La Chanze, who ages throughout the show from fourteen to her sixties! TORCH SONG TRILOGY had the first gay leading man, and THE COLOR PURPLE has the first gay leading woman.

SETH RUDETSKY WITH TONY-WINNING PLAYWRIGHT TERRENCE MCNALLY, DURING A SEGMENT OF *SETH'S CHATTERBOX*. (COURTESY OF FRANK CONWAY.)

CHAPTER TEN

Seth's Broadway Chatterbox

The actress played the lead for all three days of tech and then prepared herself to do her job and go back to the chorus. She got a call on the morning of the first preview informing her that the leading lady had gone back to New York and they were now offering her the role!

IN THE late nineties, as I got more enmeshed in the Broadway scene, I began to meet more and more people whose careers I was obsessed with. When I was first hired to play Betty Buckley's voice lesson I didn't know if this would be my only time alone with her. I spent the entire ride in her limo pumping her for scoop about CATS, THE MYSTERY OF EDWIN DROOD, and CARRIE. What was her audition like? How did she come up with that crazy high note at the end of "Writing on the Wall"? Then I was asked to interview to be the music director for Andrea Martin's one-woman show. Instead of spending the time talking myself up in order to get the job, I was barraging Andrea with questions about her brilliant characters on SCTV and her hilarious performance in MY FAVORITE YEAR. One day, David Friedman, the fantastic conductor (the Disney movies *The Little Mermaid* and *Beauty and the Beast*) and wonderful composer ("Help Is on the Way," "Listen to My Heart") saw me host a small benefit. He complimented me and said I was such a "fan." I realized he was right! I love fawning over people I was obsessed with and asking tons of questions about every aspect of the career. I decided to start my own talk show where I could find out all I wanted to know about the inside of Broadway.

Seth's Broadway Chatterbox started in December 1999 at Don't Tell Mama on Forty-sixth Street. It's a weekly show and all the money goes to BC/EFA. Not just the admission cost but also all the money raised by sales of the DVDs (www.sethsbroadwaychatterbox. com). I usually end the show by "forcing" the Broadway star I'm interviewing to sing one of their sassy signature songs. I obviously can't share that with you, but I can share my top stories!

This is my favorite story about the capriciousness of "the biz." When you think of Audrey in LITTLE SHOP OF HORRORS, you think of Ellen Greene. It almost seems like the role was written for her. It wasn't. As a matter, she wasn't the first choice for the part! When the off-Broadway show was first cast, the role of Audrey went to . . . Faith Prince! Faith was, of course, overjoyed but had a small conflict. She was under contract to do an industrial that would have conflicted with rehearsals. An industrial is a show where actors sing and dance about a particular product or company (like Coke or Rite Aid). Actors love doing these gigs because they get paid a lot for a relatively short period of time. Faith asked the industrial to let her out of her contract and replace her. They said no. She told me she still remembers getting down on her knees and begging them but they were nonplussed. That was it. She couldn't get out of the conflict and told the producers that she couldn't do the show. Of course, she wasn't totally devastated because it was only an off-Broadway show, which always pays poorly and usually doesn't run very long. The role then went to Ellen Greene, who made it her own, and instead of a short run like many off-Broadway musicals, the show became incredibly successful. LITTLE SHOP OF HORRORS eventually became a movie, and instead of hiring some famous movie actress to play Audrey, which is de rigueur in Hollwood, the film company went with Ellen. You would think that Faith has carried a chip on her shoulder for years about this vast missed opportunity, but she's completely at peace. She told me she thinks if she had played Audrey originally, she never would have been cast as Adelaide in the revival of GUYS AND DOLLS because the roles are too similar. If she hadn't played Adelaide, she never would have won her Tony

Award. So the casting worked out for both Ellen and Faith who, FYI, went on to replace Ellen in the role of Audrey. An interesting note to the story is, if Lee Wilkoff hadn't accepted the role of Seymour, it would have gone to the second choice . . . Nathan Lane! That means if Faith had done it, they would played opposite each other ten years before they were Nathan Detroit and Adelaide in GUYS AND DOLLS!

Here's my favorite story about following your instinct:

An actress I was interviewing told of how she had a final callback to play the lead in a new Broadway musical. Her agent called and told her that, unfortunately, she was offered the chorus and the understudy to the lead, but LES MIZ also called and offered her the role of Eponine! Eponine is the character who sings "On My Own" and has a fabulous death scene. The actress decided that she really believed in the new show and wanted to be a part of it. She had played Eponine on tour and wanted to do something new. Her agent reminded her that LES MIZ was offering her more money than she'd ever made and the other show was offering her chorus salary, plus it was going out of town with no guarantee of it even coming to Broadway. It didn't matter, said the actress, she believed in the show and wanted to be in it. She flew to California, against her agent's advice, and began learning her chorus track. During tech rehearsals, which are long and arduous, the producers asked her to go on for the leading lady so that she could rest before the first preview. The actress played the lead for all three days of tech and then prepared herself to do her job and go back to the chorus. She got a call on the morning of the first preview informing her that the leading lady had gone back to New York, and they were now offering *her* the role! She played it in California, took it to Broadway, and *won the Tony Award!* I'm talking about Sutton Foster in THOROUGHLY MODERN MILLIE. If she had taken her agent's advice she would have simply been an Eponine in a long line of Eponines. Instead she made the choice she felt was the most artistically satisfying to her, and it netted her a Tony Award!

The next story is one of the most embarrassing I know of to happen on a Broadway stage. Priscilla Lopez, the brilliant actress who was the original Morales in A CHORUS LINE and won the Tony Award for A DAY IN HOLLYWOOD/A NIGHT IN THE UKRAINE was in the chorus of the 1968 show, HER FIRST ROMAN. In order to wear a wig, chorus girls have to pin wig caps to their hair, and because Priscilla's hair was short, it was hard to attach the caps. She found out that if she stuffed some clothes underneath the wig cap, it would help fluff it out and make it easier for the pins to be attached. She stuffed anything she could find in her wig cap: underclothes, socks, whatever . . . it all worked. She told the other chorus girls as they were applying the leg paint to themselves that made them all look Egyptian. Many decided to take her up on her idea. Well, in Act Two there was a funeral procession where all the ladies walked in a solemn line around a coffin. Priscilla happened to look up at the dancer in front of her during the procession and saw that she had taken her advice. Unfortunately, the dancer didn't tuck all of the clothes in, and Priscilla noticed a white bra

SONGS YOU MUST DOWNLOAD

1. SONG TITLE: "Beauty School Dropout"

WHO'S SINGING: Billy Porter

SHOW: GREASE!!!! (The revival added those needy exclamation points)

WHY: Billy Porter has one of the best voices on Broadway. He played the role of the Teen Angel in the 1994 revival of GREASE starring Rosie O'Donnell. He knew he was only gonna get one big song to show off his unbelievable vocals, so he pulled out every trick in the book. He and John McDaniel (yes . . . from *The Rosie O'Donnell Show*— how do you think they met?) came up with an arrangement that goes from mellow blues to revival church gospel, all peppered with incredible Star Search riffing (Billy was a $100,000 winner). To understand the kind of singing it is, suffice it to say that Billy was replaced by . . . Jennifer Holliday!

2. SONG TITLE: "Bless the Lord"

WHO'S SINGING: Shoshanna Bean

SHOW: GODSPELL (off-Broadway 2000 revival)

WHY: Holy crap! That's what you will say when you hear this tour de force! Shoshanna had just graduated college when she got this incredibly low-paying gig at a tiny off-off-Broadway theater. The show moved officially off-Broadway and made a CD, which features such future Broadway gypsies as Barrett Foa (AVENUE Q), Chad Kimball (INTO THE WOODS), and Capathia Jenkins (Martin Short's FAME BECOMES ME). Shoshanna takes her one solo song and defies anyone to outsing her. Part Patti LuPone, part Whitney Houston, she burns up the CD. Listen how she can belt up a storm but suddenly hauls out a gorgeous soprano voice as well. Finally, she tops it all with a Mariah Carey high A above high C! No wonder she took over WICKED after Idina Menzel left the show!

3. SONG TITLE: "Meadowlark"
WHO'S SINGING: Patti LuPone
SHOW: THE BAKER'S WIFE
WHY: La LuPone can do no wrong. In THE BAKER'S WIFE she plays a young wife who leaves her older husband for a sexy young man. In "Meadowlark" she sings of her dilemma in allegory. Stephen Schwartz wrote the music and lyrics, and it's one of those Broadway songs that very few can sing because it sits at the top of most women's ranges. Listen to Patti belt out the high E on the word "pa-a-a-a-a-ast" at the end of the song. The bizarre part is that the producer, David Merrick, hated this song! As a matter of fact, he wanted it cut from the show so badly that he actually stole the music from the pit so the orchestra couldn't play it for

one performance! Thankfully, the creators won out and the song stayed. Ironically, it didn't matter because the show flopped!

4. SONG TITLE: "Memory"
WHO'S SINGING: Betty Buckley
SHOW: CATS . . . There, I said it.
WHY: Yes, we all know CATS became a big, fat joke. Andrew Lloyd Webber's tourist trap became the longest-running show due to its spectacle aspect, excellent marketing, and the fact that one didn't have to speak English to enjoy it. But, let us not forget that Betty Buckley won the Tony Award for her performance as Grizzabella. No one has ever come close to the way Betty sounds singing it. Listen how she's able to vibrato on the high E flat. It's right after the big "touch me" on the first syllable of "easy." Brava!

5. SONG TITLE: "Love Can't Happen"
WHO'S SINGING: David Carroll
SHOW: GRAND HOTEL
WHY: David Carroll's Broadway triumph was in the role of the Baron in GRAND HOTEL. Unfortunately, his HIV status made him too weak to continue doing the show eight times a week. He left the show but intended to make the album nonetheless. Unfortunately, due to infighting amongst the creators, the album was delayed for a very long time. When it was finally ready to begin, David showed

up to preserve for posterity his glorious singing of the score, but tragically he died at the recording studio. His replacement, Brent Barrett, went on to record the album. David had done his own act at a club called Steve McGraw's and closed that show with his GRAND HOTEL showstopper, "Love Can't Happen." There's a live recording of his performance as the last track on the CD, and you can hear how glorious he sounded. Pay special attention to his last note. He said it was the hardest thing he ever sang. No doubt, but it's also one of the most thrilling thing I've ever heard!

6. SONG: "Glitter and Be Gay"
WHO'S SINGING: Barbara Cook
SHOW: CANDIDE
WHY: CANDIDE has never had a long, successful run, but the score remains very popular amongst theater and classical music lovers. The young Barbara Cook plays the female lead, Cunegonde, and sings like a dream. Her unbelievable fluidity on all the scales and vocal acrobatics will make you mortified at your own voice. And that tone! It's so pure and simple and bell-like! At the end she hits a high C, then a high D-flat, then a high E-flat!!!! The song is Bernstein and Cook at their best.

7. SONG: "Unusual Way"
WHO'S SINGING: Laura Benanti
SHOW: NINE (revival)
WHY: NINE was revived with Antonio Banderas (who never missed a show) in 2003, and Laura played one of his many girlfriends. This song has one of the beautiful, haunting melodies from a Broadway show. The lyrics are mysterious and describe the familiar push and pull of an unhealthy yet intense relationship. Add to that Laura's silky soprano and ringing tone and you'll be transfixed!

8. SONG: "The Best in the World"
WHO'S SINGING: Priscilla Lopez
SHOW: A DAY IN HOLLYWOOD/A NIGHT IN THE UKRAINE
WHY When Priscilla was nominated for a Tony Award for her role as Morales, she lost to her best friend Kelly Bishop, who played Shelia. But a few years later, she won playing a Grauman's Chinese theater usher in Act One and Harpo Marx in Act Two in A DAY IN HOLLYWOOD/A NIGHT IN THE UKRAINE. The whole show was fabulous, but this particular song is a standout. It's a story song, so there's a very clear beginning, middle, and end and you can't help but feel for this usher who had dreams of silver-screen stardom. The show was mostly composed by Frank Lazarus, but this particular song is by the great Jerry Herman. Listen to the change in

melody on the third and fourth verse when Priscilla sings the word "star." I love it!

9. SONG: "Next Time/I Wouldn't Go Back"
WHO'S SINGING: Richard Muenz, Sally Mayes, Brent Barrett, Lynn Winterstellar
SHOW: CLOSER THAN EVER
WHY: CLOSER THAN EVER is dedicated to the music of David Shire and the lyrics of Richard Maltby. This particular song stands out for two reasons. First of all, everyone's voice is fab and the harmonies/chord changes are beautiful. Second of all, the lyrics are therapeutic and inspiring. The four singers express how they never expected to be where they are now (single or making a huge decision), but they realize it's exactly where they should be. It makes you excited about your own life and the possibilities that are in front of you. Plus, it sounds great!!!!!

10. SONG TITLE: "Miss Marmelstein"
WHO'S SINGING: Barbra Streisand
SHOW: I CAN GET IT FOR YOU WHOLESALE
WHY: This marked Barbra's Broadway debut at age nineteen. In the song, she's bemoaning the fact that nobody has a pithy nickname for her. They don't even call her by her first name (Yetta). No matter what, it's "Miss Marmelstein." This song was written specifically for Barbra, and she puts her mark all over it. Not only with her brilliant musical

phrasing but also her comedy chops. Listen to her right after she asks where the "lucky guy" is who will marry her. She punctuates the question with a "huh?" that makes me laugh every time I hear it!

hanging from underneath the wig and swinging freely during the solemn occasion. Priscilla wanted to laugh but of course couldn't because it was supposed to be a sad scene. She tried to suppress it, but all that did was cause incredible pressure which resulted in her finally . . . *peeing onstage!* She couldn't stop and was mortified that it was also causing her leg makeup to run in rivulets onto the stage. Soon she was even more horrified because the stage was raked. A raked stage means that the back is tilted up, and it lays in a diagonal toward the audience. Well, what comes down must go further down, apparently, because soon the pee was running downhill and overflowing from the front of the stage into the pit! I'm obsessed thinking about those poor musicians sitting in the pit wondering what was dripping on them. Hopefully, they felt some comfort in knowing it was from a future Tony Award winner!

This is my favorite story showing both the harshness and kindness of Broadway. ANNIE started up at the Goodspeed Opera House. Andrea McArdle was in it, but not as Annie—she was cast as the tough orphan, Pepper. The role of Annie went to an incredibly sweet girl named Kristin Vinegart. As rehearsals progressed, the creators realized that Annie wasn't a sweet angel, she was a tough girl from the street. They had made a mistake in casting.

What to do? They decided to put the show first and fire the young girl, no doubt traumatizing her to a degree. Andrea took over the role immediately (like most kids who perform, she had every part in the show memorized) and went on to become a Broadway star.

But what of Kristin?

A few years later, she was cast in the musical version of I REMEMBER MAMA. Thomas Meehan, who wrote the book to ANNIE, was the librettist. The show was out of town and in big trouble. Finally after a big creative staff meeting, they decided one of the roles needed to be eliminated—the role played by Kristin! That was too much for Meehan. He told them that he couldn't do that to the same girl twice. He wound up staying up all night writing her a completely *new* part so she could stay in the show! Although the show wasn't successful, it proved that people in the biz care about each other . . . sometimes!

This is the story I use to show that if you want to be a star, you have to trust yourself and go for it. There was a show called ROCK AND ROLL: THE FIRST 5,000 YEARS. It was a revue of all the greatest rock songs. Everybody in it had to imitate a famous singer, and there was one male and one female understudy. Lillias White told me she had to sing some Aretha Franklin and girl-group stuff, but all the greatest rock-and-roll singers were represented and the understudy had to do them all! Right when rehearsals began, the understudy told Lillias she was going to quit because she wanted to go into the music business. Lillias said, "Why would you do a risky thing like move to L.A. and try to become a pop star? Stay in the Broadway show and put your money in the bank.

Then, maybe, once you have a cushion, you can make the move." The understudy, though, was adamant and quit the show. Lillias couldn't understand why someone would quit a new Broadway show that had the chance to run for years. Suffice it to say that the show ran a *week* and the understudy's name was . . . Madonna!!!!!!!!

Every day something else happens on Broadway that makes a great story.

Who Started on Broadway?

#5
Q
QUIZ

1. Who starred as Tzeitel in FIDDLER ON THE ROOF?

   a. *Rosie O'Donnell*
   b. *Barbra Streisand*
   c. *Bette Midler*
   d. *Edie Gorme*

2. Who was an understudy in the original Broadway production of GREASE?

   a. *Kurt Russell*
   b. *Richard Gere*
   c. *Tom Cruise*
   d. *Gabe Kaplan*

Who Started on Broadway?

3. Who was Barbra Streisand's understudy in FUNNY GIRL?

   a. Marlo Thomas
   b. Bette Midler
   c. Doris Roberts
   d. Lainie Kazan

4. Who starred in the revivals of GREASE and HOW TO SUCCEED IN BUSINESS WITHOUT REALLY TRYING?

   a. Debra Messing
   b. Tea Leoni
   c. Megan Mullally
   d. Omarosa Manigault-Stallworth

5. Who did two Broadway musical in the early seventies?

   a. Kevin Bacon
   b. Matthew Broderick
   c. John Travolta
   d. Martha Stewart

GIVE MY REGARDS!

Conclusion

BROADWAY HAS a lot of history and a lot of scandal. But the question that always seems to come up is: Will it survive? Here are my sure-fire fixes to Broadway.

1. **BRING ON THE KIDS!** Producers need to reach out to schools across the country to make theater accessible to students. Kids need to see how wonderful theater is so they will want to continue to come to it throughout their lives. If my parents hadn't introduced me to Broadway when I was toddler, perhaps I wouldn't have started this lifelong obsession. Also, if they hadn't had such intimacy issues, perhaps I wouldn't be in lifelong therapy, but that's what we writers call a digression. Back to Broadway. When the older generation was growing up, they had the Ed Sullivan show that featured tons of Broadway performances every week, so even if you weren't from New York you knew what the latest Merman vehicle was. Nowadays, kids don't get TV exposure to Broadway, so producers have to figure out how to get Broadway to them so they can become hooked. Extra cheap tickets for school groups? Broadway people that fly around the country and perform at malls to show

the rest of the country real Broadway sass? I don't know, but we need children or Broadway will die the death of vaudeville.

2. **PRODUCERS: STOP SPENDING MONEY ON STUPID STUFF!** First of all, bring back the full orchestra. Money is frittered away on crazily expensive things like custom-made shoes and overly elaborate sets because there is a fear that audiences only want spectacle from Broadway. Audiences want music from musicals!!!! A show whose music sounds great will last longer than a show that sounds synthesized but has a set that explodes every night. The VAMPIRE LESTAT had a real fire onstage every night but fake strings. It lasted a month.

3. **AUDIENCES: STOP GIVING CRITICS SO MUCH POWER!** I know Broadway shows are expensive, but this book gives you lots of tips on how to get cheap seats. Buy tickets to many Broadway shows not just the shows the critics like. There have been so many great shows that have died because they've been killed by a handful of critics with their own agendas.

4. **GO TO OFF-BROADWAY!** Off Broadway is a place where shows can be much riskier than on Broadway because the cost is cheaper. So many fabulous shows have begun there, and if you had seen them when they first opened, you could have saved yourself the Broadway ticket price later on. Off-Broadway began the runs of AVENUE Q, A CHORUS LINE, RENT, and TORCH SONG TRILOGY. Who knows what fabulous (cheap) show is playing right now you will love!?!

5. **HAVE A VOICE!** When you see something that you think is ruining Broadway, write a letter! If you

see a critic slamming something for his/her own enjoyment, write a letter to the newspaper. If you see a Broadway show with a nine-person orchestra that charges full ticket prices, write a letter of outrage to the producers and a letter to the newspapers. If you see lip-synching on Broadway, complain! Likewise, if you like something, write a fan letter. It makes everyone involved in a show feel great to personally know people like it. For every Broadway show I've worked on, there have been a handful of fan letters posted near the sign-in board that inspire the cast and crew to go out and do a great show. It means a lot to read how a person loved a particular performance or theme or song. Or book.

6. **GO SEE A SHOW WITH NO STARS.** One of the main things people complain about is the influx of Hollywood/TV stars who are being trotted out to star in shows they're not suited for. That's because audiences are too scared to spend their money on a show without a familiar name. But why is the name of an eighties sitcom star assurance the show will be good? It's usually just assurance that their TV show was cancelled for a reason. Start a trend and go see shows that don't have anybody from *One Day at a Time* starring in it. You'll be surprised at how talented "unknown" actors can be. (Although I do love Ann, Barbara, and Julie! And Schneider! Cute!)

7. **STOP BEING ASHAMED OF LOVING BROADWAY!** Why are gay theater fanatics called "show queens" which has a derogatory inflection? Do straight men who love sports have a derogatory name for themselves? Of course not, they're straight. Nothing they enjoy

could ever be considered uncool. Here's the thing to remember, if you're gay and you love theater, it's because you're smart and you have good taste.

The question again is: Will Broadway survive? The answer is: It will if we want it to! Now, go to TalkinBroadway.com and post something, or listen to your newest Broadway CD and sing along, or write a new play that you want to see produced on Broadway. Do everything you can to keep theater alive!

ANSWERS TO QUIZZES

Quiz #1: Know Your Sondheim

1: B. Oscar Hammerstein lived near Sondheim's childhood vacation house and gave Sondheim his earliest lessons in how to write a show. Later Sondheim took over his mentor's place when he wrote DO I HEAR A WALTZ? with Richard Rodgers.

2. ANYONE CAN WHISTLE and SWEENEY TODD

3. Len Cariou, Bob Gunton, and Michael Cerveris

4. THE FROGS. Also, Nathan Lane's costar was Chris Kattan from *Saturday Night Live*, who was replaced before opening by Roger Bart.

5. A. Elizabeth Taylor. Her next biggest mistake was Larry Fortensky.

Q Quiz #2: Know Your Classic Musicals

1. C. From MY FAIR LADY and CAMELOT

2. B. Read all about it in her autobiography *Call Me Shirley.*

3. C. She originated GYPSY and CALL ME MADAM . . .

and was a replacement Dolly!

4. D. Nancy Walker started out on Broadway but achieved much of her fame as Ida Morgenstern on *The Mary Tyler Moore Show* and then *Rhoda*. Also, as the Bounty lady . . . it's "the quicker picker upper!"

5. B. John Raitt . . . also the father of Bonnie Raitt!

Q Quiz #3:
Which Actor/Which Version?

1. Carol Lawrence and Natalie Wood
2. Chita Rivera, Bebe Neuwirth, and Catherine Zeta-Jones
3. Divine, Harvey Fierstein, and John Travolta
4. Daphne Rubin-Vega and Rosario Dawson
5. Ethel Merman, Rosalind Russell, Angela Lansbury, Tyne Daly, Bette Midler, and Bernadette Peters.

Q Quiz #4:
Know Your Divas

1. B. Betty Lynn is her real name, and that's what her friends call her. FYI: Her mom's name is Betty Bob!

2. C. Her name is Donna DeSeta.

3. B. His name is Robert LuPone, and he was nominated for a Tony Award for his role in A CHORUS LINE.

4. A. She was able to give that heart-wrenching performance at the age of twenty-one!!!!

5. Chita Rivera! Chita has starred in Broadway shows every decade since the 1950s!

Q Quiz #5:
Who Started On Broadway?

1. C. She can be seen on the 1969 Tony Awards. She's fabulous even back then!
2. B. And, according to a cast member, even when Richard would go on for Eugene, the nerd, he would get tons of fan mail because his sexiness shined through!
3. D. When Lainie went on for the first time, she sent out numerous press releases even though she barely had any notice. Critics came to see her, and although the reviews weren't glowing, they weren't terrible. Barbra allegedly was quite cold to Lainie from then on and soon Lainie "quit" the show. The next Fanny understudy had a stipulation in her contract that, should she go on, she was not allowed to contact the press. Don't upstage La Streisand!
4. C. She also understudied Rosie O'Donnell as Rizzo and went on!
5. C. He was in OVER HERE and GREASE before he became Vinnie Barbarino in *Welcome Back, Kotter* and shot to stardom.

ACKNOWLEDGMENTS

I'd like to thank—

Aaron Dai, for his continual love and support...and for letting me use the computer.

Tim Cross and Jack Plotnick, for giving me their brava feedback while I was writing this book.

My excellent agent, Eric Myers, who shmoozed me to Joe Pittman, who created the fabulous Q Guide series.

My sassy family, for introducing me to music and Broadway.

...and Maggie, for being a good girl!